Dave Perry

Dave Perry's 100 Best Racing Rules Quizzes

Based on
*The Racing Rules
of Sailing for 2009–2012*

FOURTH EDITION

T0204502

OTHER BOOKS BY DAVE PERRY

Winning in One-Designs

Understanding the Racing Rules of Sailing

The author and the United States Sailing Association give permission for these Rules Quizzes and their accompanying illustrations to be reprinted for educational or entertainment value provided they are not for resale and are accompanied in print with the words: "Answers are based on *The Racing Rules of Sailing for 2009–2012. Dave Perry's 100 Best Racing Rules Quizzes* is published by the United States Sailing Association (US SAILING). For a comprehensive explanation of the rules, read Dave Perry's *Understanding the Racing Rules of Sailing through 2012* which also is available from US SAILING — 1 (800) 877-2451 or www.ussailing.org"

TO CONTACT US SAILING

PO Box 1260, 15 Maritime Drive
Portsmouth, RI 02871 USA

Phone: 401 683-0800
Fax: 401 683-0840

info@ussailing.org
www.ussailing.org

ISBN 978-0-9821676-0-1

Published by the United States Sailing Association
© 2008 by the United States Sailing Association and Dave Perry

The Racing Rules of Sailing for 2009–2012 © 2008
by the International Sailing Federation (ISAF)

FOURTH EDITION
Previously published in 1994, 1998 and 2005

Diagrams by Joy Shipman

Cover photograph of Melges 32's at Acura Key West Race Week 2007
© Andy Newman

Contents

Preface

IT WAS MY PLEASURE TO WRITE the monthly *Dave Perry's Rules Quiz* for US SAILING's magazine, then entitled *American Sailor*. In 1994, I compiled 100 of the Rules Quizzes into the first edition of *Dave Perry's 100 Best Racing Rules Quizzes*; and in 2005 I updated the Quizzes to the 2005-2008 *Racing Rules of Sailing*. My rules interest and enjoyment began when my father, Hop Perry, used to make up situations for me to solve around the dinner table. I was twelve years old. My love of solving rules quizzes is just as strong today, and judging from the popularity of the monthly Rules Quiz in *American Sailor*, and of the first three editions of this book, that love is shared by many sailors nationwide.

In this edition, I have included some features that are intended to make the book even more helpful and fun. In addition to updating each quiz to the 2009-2012 *Racing Rules of Sailing*, I have included an Advanced Rules Quiz section, two indexes that will help you find quizzes by subject and rule number, and I have included a great piece written by Bill Ficker on how to prepare for and be successful in a protest hearing.

My rules knowledge increased tremendously when I began sitting on protest committees and hearing protests. Through the enjoyable Rules Quiz format, in which you are cast as a member of a protest or appeals committee, it is hoped that your rules knowledge and clarity will increase also. As you become more familiar with the rules, you will gain more confidence in your tactics and your close-quarters maneuvering, and your racing will dramatically improve. I also hope this will encourage you to volunteer to sit on an actual protest committee. You can initially ask to be a silent observer. Then as you gain confidence and experience you will soon become a voting member and begin giving back to the sport in a very significant and enjoyable way.

My strong recommendation, as you go through this book, is to keep in mind the great advice I received from Bill Bentsen, long time member of the US SAIL-ING and ISAF Racing Rules Committees, who said: "Before answering a rules question, I always reread the rule first." Rules knowledge is not a closed book exam. The best judges will open their rulebook during a protest hearing to be sure they get it right. I strongly encourage you to have a rulebook with you as you work through these quizzes; and to open it frequently to review or read the rules that are referred to.

Also, because the US SAILING Appeals Book and ISAF Case Book are on-line at www.ussailing.org/appeals, be sure to read each Appeal and Case referenced in these quizzes.

Please note that the scenarios in this book are primarily fleet racing situations. The appendices in *The Racing Rules of Sailing* for racing windsurfers, radio-controlled model yachts, and for team and match racing sometimes change the racing rules in the main body of the book. In some instances, I refer to those changes in the Answer. But be sure to read the appendices carefully when racing in those special disciplines.

Also note: there may be scenarios in these quizzes in which you feel that a protest is not justified based on good sportsmanship. It is important to keep in mind that these quizzes are solely focusing on what the racing rules say, and are not recommendations for action. They are designed solely to highlight a specific aspect of a racing rule.

Finally, I wish to point out that my opinions expressed in this book are my personal opinions, and not those of the US SAILING Appeals Committee of which I am a member.

For encouraging me to undertake this book, I want to acknowledge Jerry Daly; his friendly insistence paid off. For all their time and expertise in reviewing these quizzes over the years, I want to acknowledge and thank Bill Bentsen, Harman Hawkins and Dick Rose. For writing such excellent advice for preparing for a protest hearing, I want to thank Bill Ficker and Mary Savage who updated Bill's original work to the new rules. And I want to acknowledge and thank Joy Shipman who designed this book.

As these Rules Quizzes are excellent educational tools for class newsletters, junior and other instructional programs, judges seminars, etc. I give my permission for the reprint* of these quizzes as they appear in this book provided they are not for resale.

And now, go ahead and see how you would decide these protests and appeals, and enjoy!

Dave Perry

* Please annotate any reprint of these quizzes with the following:

"Answers are based on *The Racing Rules of Sailing for 2009–2012. Dave Perry's 100 Best Racing Rules Quizzes* is published by the United States Sailing Association (US SAILING). For a comprehensive explanation of the rules, read Dave Perry's *Understanding the Racing Rules of Sailing through 2012* which also is available from US SAILING — 1 (800) 877-2451 or www.ussailing.org"

Quizzes 1-5

Introduction, Definitions and the rules of Part 1

WIND

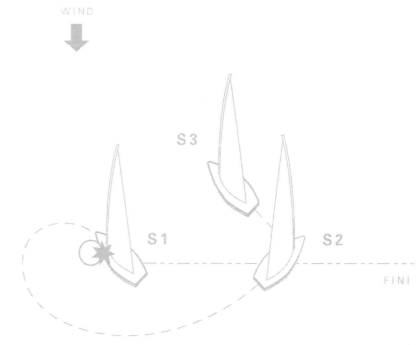

Quiz 1

How often are the *The Racing Rules of Sailing* revised; and what is the process for revising them?

ANSWER

Beginning with the 1965-1968 edition, *The Racing Rules of Sailing* (RRS) have been revised every four years to go into effect the year following the Olympic Regatta.

Throughout the four year period between revisions, the racing rules committees (RRC) of the member national authorities (MNA) around the world study the rules for areas of improvement and draft possible rule changes for review. Sailors in each country are welcomed to communicate their ideas to their RRC. The RRCs then submit their suggestions for changes to the International Sailing Federation Racing Rules Committee (ISAF RRC) for their consideration. Each member national authority RRC has the opportunity to review the submissions from the other member national authorities.

In the year of the Olympic Regatta ISAF adopts a new edition of the RRS. Each member national authority then adds their prescriptions to the RRS, and the new edition typically goes into effect on January 1 of the following year.

Answers are based on *The Racing Rules of Sailing for 2009 – 2012*. *Dave Perry's 100 Best Racing Rules Quizzes* is published by the United States Sailing Association (US SAILING). For a comprehensive explanation of the rules, read Dave Perry's *Understanding the Racing Rules of Sailing through 2012* which also is available from US SAILING — 1 (800) 877-2451 or www.ussailing.org

Quiz 2

A more experienced helmsman of a port-tack boat (P) hails, "Starboard!" to a beginner who, although on starboard tack, not being sure of himself and worried about having his boat holed, tacks to port tack to avoid a collision. A third boat in the race protests the situation. You are on the protest committee; how would you decide this?

ANSWER

Boat P is penalized under rule 2, Fair Sailing. Rule 60.1, Right to Protest; Right to Request Redress or Rule 69 Action, permits a third boat to protest an incident involving other boats. A boat that deliberately hails "Starboard" when she is on port tack has not acted "in compliance with recognized principles of sportsmanship and fair play." (See ISAF Case 47.)

Answers are based on *The Racing Rules of Sailing for 2009 – 2012. Dave Perry's 100 Best Racing Rules Quizzes* is published by the United States Sailing Association (US SAILING). For a comprehensive explanation of the rules, read Dave Perry's *Understanding the Racing Rules of Sailing through 2012* which also is available from US SAILING — 1 (800) 877-2451 or www.ussailing.org

Quiz 3

Boat S (on starboard tack) touches the finishing mark on her leeward side, bears away, gybes, then immediately re-crosses the finishing line on port tack and tacks to starboard tack. Ashore, S reads in the race results that the race committee has scored her 'Did not finish.' She requests redress under rule 62.1(a), Redress, and in the hearing claims that she sailed the course, took her penalty and finished correctly. You are on the protest committee; how would you decide this?

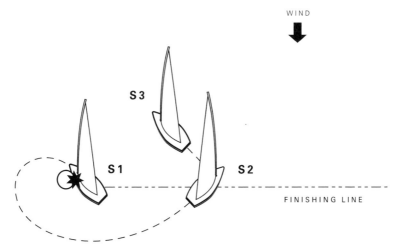

ANSWER

Uphold the scoring of the race committee. Rule 44.2, Penalties at the Time of an Incident, requires that a boat taking a penalty after touching a finishing mark return completely to the course side of the finishing line before finishing. Boat S took her penalty by making one turn that included a gybe and a tack, but she failed to then sail completely to the course side of the finishing line before crossing it, and as a result she did not finish (see the definition Finish). Rule A5, Scores Determined by the Race Committee, permits the race committee to score a boat 'Did not finish' without protesting her or holding a hearing.

Answers are based on *The Racing Rules of Sailing for 2009 – 2012. Dave Perry's 100 Best Racing Rules Quizzes* is published by the United States Sailing Association (US SAILING). For a comprehensive explanation of the rules, read Dave Perry's *Understanding the Racing Rules of Sailing through 2012* which also is available from US SAILING — 1 (800) 877-2451 or www.ussailing.org

Quiz 4

Boats X and Y, on a downwind leg, are converging on steady courses for ten seconds. X is to Y's right (looking downwind), and is sailing on port tack with the wind directly astern and her boom on her starboard side. Y is sailing "by the lee" with the wind coming over her starboard stern quarter and her boom also on the starboard side. They have contact with no damage or injury, and both protest. You are on the protest committee; how would you decide this?

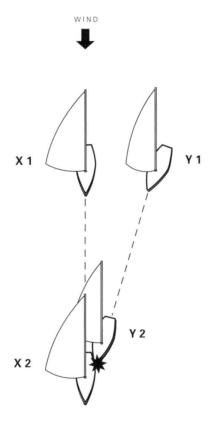

Answers are based on *The Racing Rules of Sailing for 2009 – 2012. Dave Perry's 100 Best Racing Rules Quizzes* is published by the United States Sailing Association (US SAILING). For a comprehensive explanation of the rules, read Dave Perry's *Understanding the Racing Rules of Sailing through 2012* which also is available from US SAILING — 1 (800) 877-2451 or www.ussailing.org

ANSWER

Boat Y is penalized for breaking rule 11, On the Same Tack, Overlapped. Whether a boat is on port or starboard tack is determined by her windward side (see definition Tack, Starboard or Port which refers to the definition Leeward and Windward). The leeward side of a boat is the side that is or, when she is head to wind, was away from the wind. However, when sailing directly downwind or by the lee (i.e., with the wind coming over her stern from the same side on which she is carrying her mainsail), her leeward side is the side on which her mainsail lies. The opposite side is the windward side. Y has the wind coming over her stern from the same side that her mainsail is on (starboard), so the windward side is the other side (port). Therefore she and X are both on port tack; and as the windward boat, Y is required to keep clear under rule 11.

Y also broke rule 14, Avoiding Contact, because it was possible for her to have avoided hitting X. Whether or not X could have avoided contact when it was clear to her that Y was not going to keep clear is a moot point. X, as the right-of-way boat, can only be penalized under rule 14 if the contact results in damage or injury [see rule 14(b)].

Answers are based on *The Racing Rules of Sailing for 2009–2012. Dave Perry's 100 Best Racing Rules Quizzes* is published by the United States Sailing Association (US SAILING). For a comprehensive explanation of the rules, read Dave Perry's *Understanding the Racing Rules of Sailing through 2012* which also is available from US SAILING — 1 (800) 877-2451 or www.ussailing.org

Quiz 5

A race committee boat is anchored at the port end of the starting line. Boat X starts and immediately catches the race committee boat's anchor line on her centerboard. Reacting quickly, X's helmsman heels the boat while her crew goes to leeward, pushes the anchor line down and frees it from the centerboard. X does not touch the committee boat, nor does she do a turn after the incident. Boat Y protests. You are on the protest committee; how would you decide this?

ANSWER

Boat Y's protest is disallowed. X does not break rule 31, Touching a Mark, because she does not touch the mark. The definition Mark reads, "An anchor line and objects attached temporarily or accidentally to a mark are not part of it." Furthermore, X does not propel herself by pulling on the anchor line; therefore she does not break rule 42, Propulsion.

Answers are based on *The Racing Rules of Sailing for 2009 – 2012*. *Dave Perry's 100 Best Racing Rules Quizzes* is published by the United States Sailing Association (US SAILING). For a comprehensive explanation of the rules, read Dave Perry's *Understanding the Racing Rules of Sailing through 2012* which also is available from US SAILING — 1 (800) 877-2451 or www.ussailing.org

Quizzes 6-29

The rules of Part 2, Sections A and B

When Boats Meet: Right of Way and General Limitations

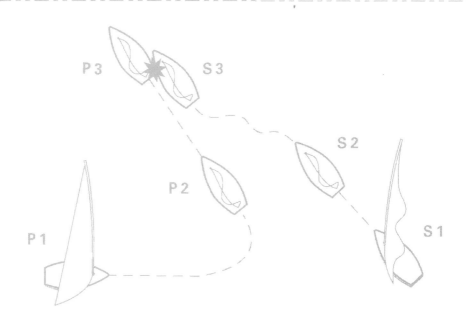

Quiz 6

Boats S (on starboard tack) and P (on port tack), both close-hauled, are converging on a beat. P will safely cross S. However, when they are less than two lengths apart, the wind veers (shifts to the right) ten degrees. S luffs (changes her course) in response to the windshift, such that P is unable to keep clear. There is minor contact with no damage or injury, and both boats protest. You are on the protest committee; how would you decide this?

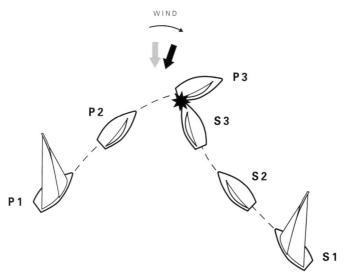

ANSWER

Boat S is penalized under rule 16.1, Changing Course. Rule 16.1 states, "When a right-of-way boat changes course, she shall give the other boat room to keep clear." S changes course when so close to P that P is unable to keep clear and there is contact. Therefore, S failed to give P room to keep clear, thereby breaking rule 16.1. S also broke rule 14, Avoiding Contact; but as the right-of-way boat, she can only be penalized under rule 14 if the contact results in damage or injury [see rule 14(b)]. P did not break rule 14, because S changed course so close to P that it was not possible for P to avoid the contact.

Answers are based on *The Racing Rules of Sailing for 2009 – 2012. Dave Perry's 100 Best Racing Rules Quizzes* is published by the United States Sailing Association (US SAILING). For a comprehensive explanation of the rules, read Dave Perry's *Understanding the Racing Rules of Sailing through 2012* which also is available from US SAILING — 1 (800) 877-2451 or www.ussailing.org

Quiz 7

Boat P (on port tack) and Boat S (on starboard tack), sailing close-hauled, are converging on a collision course. When three lengths apart, P bears away in order to pass astern of S. When two lengths apart, S tacks, during which time P holds her course. After S is on a close-hauled course, P luffs to her close-hauled course to avoid hitting S, and protests S under rules 16.1 and 16.2, Changing Course, and 13, While Tacking. You are on the protest committee; how would you decide this?

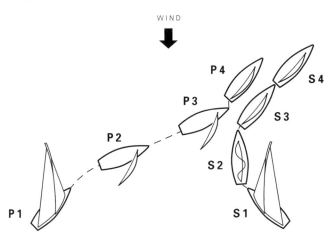

ANSWER

Boat P's protest is disallowed. As Boat S luffs in preparation to tacking, P does not need to change her course to continue to keep clear of S; therefore S complies with rules 16.1 and 16.2. Similarly, while S is past head to wind but before on a close-hauled course, P does not have to change course to avoid a collision with S; therefore S complies with rule 13. After S is on a close-hauled course, i.e., completes her tack, she becomes the right-of-way boat (as the leeward boat) and P is able to keep clear of S, which she demonstrates by her actual performance. Therefore S complies with rule 15, Acquiring Right of Way, and P complies with rule 11, On the Same Tack, Overlapped. The action of P, in bearing away, does not of itself require S to maintain her course. In this case, neither boat broke a rule.

Answers are based on *The Racing Rules of Sailing for 2009 – 2012*. *Dave Perry's 100 Best Racing Rules Quizzes* is published by the United States Sailing Association (US SAILING). For a comprehensive explanation of the rules, read Dave Perry's *Understanding the Racing Rules of Sailing through 2012* which also is available from US SAILING — 1 (800) 877-2451 or www.ussailing.org

Quiz 8

Boat S (on starboard tack) is close-hauled and Boat P (on port tack) is broad reaching on a course taking her clear to windward of S. When they are approximately two lengths apart, a gust strikes S and she rounds up out of control and collides with P. The protest committee finds in favor of S, concluding that in the gusting conditions P should have kept far enough away to enable her to change course to avoid the collision caused by S's rounding up. P appeals this decision. You are on the appeals committee; how would you decide this?

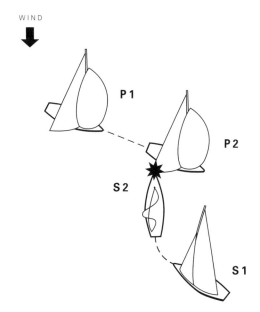

ANSWER

The protest committee decision is reversed and Boat S is penalized for breaking rule 16.1, Changing Course. Rule 16.1 requires that when a right-of-way boat changes her course, she give the keep-clear boat room to keep clear. No rule obligates P to anticipate a sudden course change by S. The fact that S's change of course was unintentional is not relevant to the application of rule 16.1.

Answers are based on *The Racing Rules of Sailing for 2009 – 2012. Dave Perry's 100 Best Racing Rules Quizzes* is published by the United States Sailing Association (US SAILING). For a comprehensive explanation of the rules, read Dave Perry's *Understanding the Racing Rules of Sailing through 2012* which also is available from US SAILING — 1 (800) 877-2451 or www.ussailing.org

Quiz 9

Boats P (on port tack) and S (on starboard tack) are sailing up a beat on op-posite tacks on a collision course. As they get closer, S hails, "Starboard!" and P hails, "Hold your course!" S then bears away and passes within a few feet of P's stern. Both boats protest. You are on the protest committee; how would you decide this?

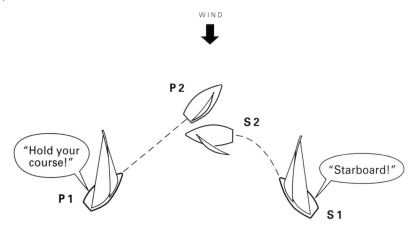

ANSWER

Boat P is penalized under rule 10, On Opposite Tacks. P's hail of "Hold your course" is permissible, but the rules do not recognize such a hail as binding on the other boat. S can and should take avoiding action when she needs to in order to avoid a collision. (See US SAILING Appeal 27.)

Answers are based on *The Racing Rules of Sailing for 2009 – 2012. Dave Perry's 100 Best Racing Rules Quizzes* is published by the United States Sailing Association (US SAILING). For a comprehensive explanation of the rules, read Dave Perry's *Understanding the Racing Rules of Sailing through 2012* which also is available from US SAILING — 1 (800) 877-2451 or www.ussailing.org

Quiz 10

Boats X and Y are sailing dead-downwind halfway down a run. X, whose boom is out over her port side, is clear astern of Y, whose boom is out over her starboard side. X is blanketing Y's wind and is catching up quickly. Neither boat has changed her course in the 10 or so lengths preceding the incident. X finally catches up and her bow makes contact with Y's transom. There is no damage or injury. Both protest each other. You are on the protest committee; how would you decide this?

WIND

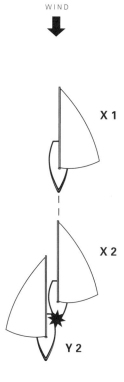

ANSWER

Boat Y is penalized under rules 10, On Opposite Tacks and 14, Avoiding Contact. X is on starboard tack and Y is on port tack (see definition Tack, Starboard or Port). The right-of-way rule for two boats on opposite tacks is rule 10, "... a port-tack boat shall keep clear of a starboard-tack boat." Y failed to keep clear and so breaks rule 10. Rule 12, On the Same Tack, Not Overlapped, pertaining to boats clear ahead and clear astern, applies only when the boats are on the same tack. Regarding the collision, rule 14, Avoiding Contact, requires all boats to avoid contact when reasonably possible. Certainly X could have avoided Y, but didn't; therefore she breaks rule 14. But a right-of-way boat can be penalized under rule 14 only when damage or injury results from the collision [rule 14(b)]. In this case there was neither.

Y also could have avoided the contact by moving off of X's course.

Answers are based on *The Racing Rules of Sailing for 2009 – 2012. Dave Perry's 100 Best Racing Rules Quizzes* is published by the United States Sailing Association (US SAILING). For a comprehensive explanation of the rules, read Dave Perry's *Understanding the Racing Rules of Sailing through 2012* which also is available from US SAILING — 1 (800) 877-2451 or www.ussailing.org

Quiz 11

Boats S and P, two close-hauled dinghies, are approaching each other on a collision course in medium breeze. P fails to keep clear and S bears away to pass astern of P. As she passes astern of P, S accidentally hits the starboard corner of P's transom, putting a small crack in S's bow and a 12-inch scratch along her starboard bow. She is safely able to continue in the race. P immediately does a Two-Turns Penalty and protests S. You are on the protest committee; how would you decide this?

ANSWER

Boat S is penalized for breaking rule 14, Avoiding Contact. Given that she "accidentally" hit P, the presumption is that it was "reasonably possible" for her to have avoided contact with P had she been more careful. However, S, as a right-of-way boat, cannot be penalized for breaking rule 14 unless the contact causes damage or injury to either boat. In this case, S was damaged and therefore she is penalized for breaking rule 14. She could have exonerated herself by doing a Two-Turns Penalty, but she failed to do so leaving disqualification as the only penalty available to the protest committee (rule 64.1(a), Penalties and Exoneration).

Answers are based on *The Racing Rules of Sailing for 2009 – 2012*. *Dave Perry's 100 Best Racing Rules Quizzes* is published by the United States Sailing Association (US SAILING). For a comprehensive explanation of the rules, read Dave Perry's *Understanding the Racing Rules of Sailing through 2012* which also is available from US SAILING — 1 (800) 877-2451 or www.ussailing.org

Quiz 12

Boats L (a leeward boat) and W (a windward boat) are approaching the starting line shortly before the starting signal. Both are on starboard tack with W
near close-hauled and sailing slowly. L becomes overlapped not far to leeward
of W from clear astern. The two boats sail for a few seconds, on parallel
courses. L then hails her intention to luff. W immediately reacts by shoving her
helm hard to leeward and tacking. During her maneuver, the port corner of
W's transom contacts L near amidships. In her protest, W claims that L became
overlapped too close thereby denying W of "room to keep clear" as required
by rule 15, Acquiring Right of Way. The protest committee finds that when L
became overlapped, W was in fact keeping clear because the boats were not
on a collision course and because L would not immediately hit W if L changed
course (see definition Keep Clear). The PC further finds that W had enough
room to luff away from L provided she luffed slowly. W is penalized for breaking rule 11 (a windward boat shall keep clear of a leeward boat). W appeals,
claiming that she isn't required to take any avoiding action until L announces
her intention to luff; and at that point she is entitled to room to tack away if
she needs it. You are on the appeals committee; how would you decide this?

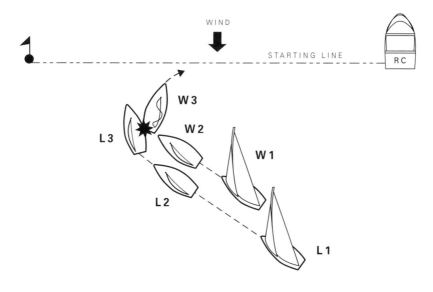

Answers are based on *The Racing Rules of Sailing for 2009–2012. Dave Perry's 100 Best Racing Rules Quizzes* is published by the
United States Sailing Association (US SAILING). For a comprehensive explanation of the rules, read Dave Perry's *Understanding
the Racing Rules of Sailing through 2012* which also is available from US SAILING — 1 (800) 877-2451 or www.ussailing.org

ANSWER TO QUIZ 12

The appeal is denied; Boat W is penalized for breaking rule 11, On the Same Tack, Overlapped. When L becomes overlapped to leeward of W, she is initially obligated by rule 15 to give W room to keep clear. This she does, shown by the fact that thereafter the boats sail parallel courses without contact, and that L would not immediately hit W if L luffed or bore away. Had L luffed, she would have been subject to the limitations of rule 16.1, Changing Course, which requires her to give W the room necessary to respond. A windward boat's right to "room to keep clear" under rules 15 and 16.1 is a shield, not a sword for W. L did not luff (her hail is immaterial) and W made an unnecessarily extreme luff and hit L. (See US SAILING Appeal 43.)

Answers are based on *The Racing Rules of Sailing for 2009 – 2012*. *Dave Perry's 100 Best Racing Rules Quizzes* is published by the United States Sailing Association (US SAILING). For a comprehensive explanation of the rules, read Dave Perry's *Understanding the Racing Rules of Sailing through 2012* which also is available from US SAILING — 1 (800) 877-2451 or www.ussailing.org

Quiz 13

With 45 seconds to go before the starting signal, Boat P (on port tack) on a beam reach, is approaching Boat S (on starboard tack) who is sitting nearly wayless on a close-hauled course with her sails luffing. P proceeds to luff and then cross head to wind all in one motion, ending up to leeward of S. When on a parallel course with S, P stops her change of course, never filling her sails. S, despite having room to get steerageway on and to keep clear, chooses to make no attempt to keep clear of P and 15 seconds later drifts down and makes contact (no damage or injury) with P. Both boats protest, S claiming that P had not completed her tack because she tacked from a reach and never filled her sails. You are on the protest committee; how would you decide this?

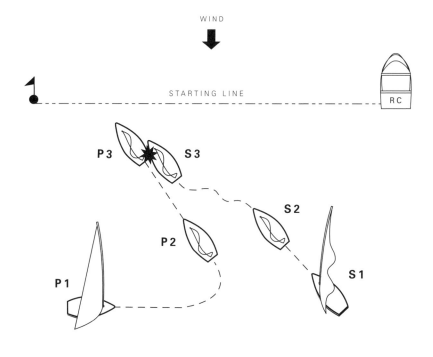

Answers are based on *The Racing Rules of Sailing for 2009 – 2012. Dave Perry's 100 Best Racing Rules Quizzes* is published by the United States Sailing Association (US SAILING). For a comprehensive explanation of the rules, read Dave Perry's *Understanding the Racing Rules of Sailing through 2012* which also is available from US SAILING — 1 (800) 877-2451 or www.ussailing.org

ANSWER TO QUIZ 13

Boat S is penalized for breaking rule 11, On the Same Tack, Overlapped, which says, "When boats are on the same tack and overlapped, a windward boat shall keep clear of a leeward boat." Once she is past head to wind, rule 13 requires P to keep clear of S until P is on a close-hauled course. When she has borne away to a close-hauled course (the course she will sail when close-hauled), P becomes the right-of-way boat under rule 11 regardless of her point of sail prior to the tack or whether her sails have filled or not after the tack. At that point, rule 15, Acquiring Right of Way, builds in a short period of time during which P, the new right-of-way boat, must give S, the new keep-clear boat, room to keep clear. S makes no effort at all to keep clear and substantial time passes prior to the contact. Therefore S, as the windward boat, is penalized for failing to keep clear of P, the leeward boat. S also broke rule 14 by failing to avoid contact.

S also broke rule 14, Avoiding Contact, because it was possible for her to have avoided hitting P. Whether or not P could have avoided contact when it was clear to her that S was not going to keep clear is a moot point. P, as the right-of-way boat, can only be penalized under rule 14 if the contact results in damage or injury [see rule 14(b)].

Answers are based on *The Racing Rules of Sailing for 2009–2012. Dave Perry's 100 Best Racing Rules Quizzes* is published by the United States Sailing Association (US SAILING). For a comprehensive explanation of the rules, read Dave Perry's *Understanding the Racing Rules of Sailing through 2012* which also is available from US SAILING — 1 (800) 877-2451 or www.ussailing.org

Quiz 14

With 30 seconds to go before the starting signal, Boat P (on port tack) on a beam reach, is approaching Boat S (on starboard tack) who is on a close-hauled course. P proceeds to luff and then cross head to wind all in one motion, ending up to leeward of S. Just after P passes head to wind she holds her course, telling S to keep clear because she is on starboard tack and a leeward boat. S luffs to avoid contact with P and protests. You are on the protest committee; how would you decide this?

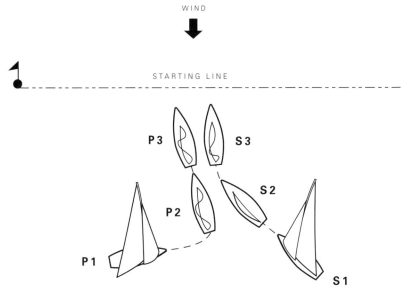

ANSWER

Boat P is penalized under rule 13, While Tacking. When P passes head to wind, she changes tack from port tack to starboard tack. However, rule 13 states that after a boat passes head to wind, she must keep clear of other boats until she is on a close-hauled course; and before she gets to close-hauled, rules 10, 11 and 12 do not apply. Rule 11, On the Same Tack, Overlapped, is the windward/ leeward rule. P has not borne away to a close-hauled course when S has to change course to avoid contact; therefore P breaks rule 13.

Answers are based on *The Racing Rules of Sailing for 2009 – 2012. Dave Perry's 100 Best Racing Rules Quizzes* is published by the United States Sailing Association (US SAILING). For a comprehensive explanation of the rules, read Dave Perry's *Understanding the Racing Rules of Sailing through 2012* which also is available from US SAILING — 1 (800) 877-2451 or www.ussailing.org

Quiz 15

Thirty seconds before the starting signal, Boat W is nearly wayless, her sails flapping. About one length prior to becoming overlapped to leeward, Boat L hails, "Leeward boat." W takes no evasive action. Two seconds after L becomes overlapped to leeward of W, L has to bear away to avoid contact with W. W begins trimming her sails and heading up immediately after the overlap is established. L protests. The protest committee finds that W, having been given adequate warning of the impending situation, fails to keep clear of a leeward boat, thereby breaking rule 11, On the Same Tack, Overlapped. W appeals. You are on the appeals committee; how would you decide this?

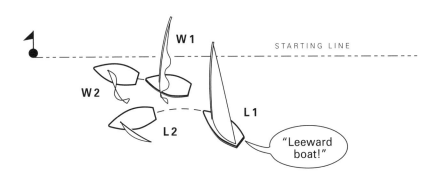

ANSWER

Boat W's appeal is sustained; neither boat broke any rule. Adequate time for response is incorporated into rule 15, Acquiring Right of Way, by its requirement to allow a newly obligated boat "room to keep clear." This rule does not require a boat clear ahead to anticipate her requirement to keep clear as a windward boat before the boat clear astern becomes overlapped to leeward. When L becomes overlapped and therefore the right-of-way boat, rule 15 requires her to give W "room to keep clear." If L doesn't bear away and avoid W as W is maneuvering to keep clear, she breaks rule 15. And, since W at once trims her sails, heads up, and thereafter keeps clear, she fulfills her obligation under rule 11. (See ISAF Case 53.)

Answers are based on *The Racing Rules of Sailing for 2009 – 2012. Dave Perry's 100 Best Racing Rules Quizzes* is published by the United States Sailing Association (US SAILING). For a comprehensive explanation of the rules, read Dave Perry's *Understanding the Racing Rules of Sailing through 2012* which also is available from US SAILING — 1 (800) 877-2451 or www.ussailing.org

Quiz 16

Two 25-foot boats, L (a leeward boat) and W (a windward boat), are approaching the right-hand end of the starting line, a 30-foot powerboat, to start an upwind leg. Both boats are beam reaching, with L on a course to pass one length to leeward of the race committee boat. Twenty seconds before the starting signal and when two lengths from the race committee boat, L hails, "No room" to W. Both boats hold their courses until W is overlapped to leeward of the race committee boat. At that point L luffs and W makes contact nearly simultaneously with both L and the committee boat. There is damage to W but not serious damage. Both boats protest each other. You are on the protest committee; how would you decide this?

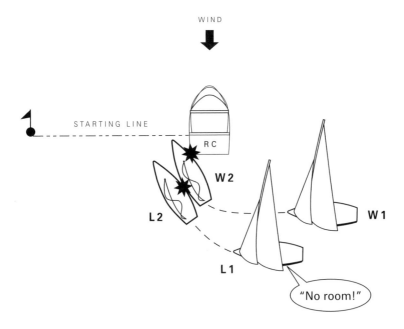

ANSWER

Boat L is penalized under rules 14, Avoiding Contact and 16.1, Changing Course. The preamble to Section C, At Marks and Obstructions, states that rule 18 does not apply "at a starting mark surrounded by navigable water or at its anchor line from the time the boats are approaching them to start..." Therefore the situation is governed by the rules in Sections A and B. At the time W becomes overlapped to leeward of the race committee boat, she is keeping clear of L in compliance with rule 11, On the Same Tack, Overlapped. Rule 16.1, Changing Course, requires L, as a right-of-way boat, to give W room to keep clear of her when she changes her course. When L luffs, there is not room for W to keep clear due to the physical presence of the race committee boat. Therefore L breaks rule 16.1. Had L wished to prevent W from passing between her and the committee boat, she should have luffed sooner while W was still able to respond to her luff. L also breaks rule 14 for failing to avoid a collision; and is penalized under that rule because the contact resulted in damage. However, from the time L began to luff, it was not possible for W to avoid contact; therefore she did not break rule 14.

Answers are based on *The Racing Rules of Sailing for 2009 – 2012. Dave Perry's 100 Best Racing Rules Quizzes* is published by the United States Sailing Association (US SAILING). For a comprehensive explanation of the rules, read Dave Perry's *Understanding the Racing Rules of Sailing through 2012* which also is available from US SAILING — 1 (800) 877-2451 or www.ussailing.org

Quiz 17

Two 25-foot boats, L (a leeward boat) and W (a windward boat), are approaching the right-hand end of the starting line, a 30-foot powerboat, to start an upwind leg. L has come in from clear astern within a length of W. Both boats are sailing close-hauled and L is overlapped by about two feet on W and on a course to pass one length to the left of the race committee boat. Ten seconds before the starting signal and when two lengths from the race committee boat, L hails to W, "No room, you're barging!" L then slowly luffs head to wind, W makes no attempt to get away from L though there is space and time for her to do so, and there is contact with no damage or injury. Both boats protest each other. You are on the protest committee; how would you decide this?

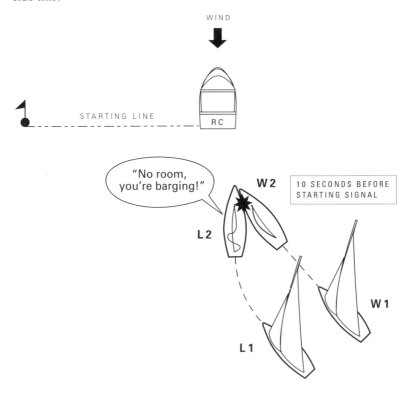

Answers are based on *The Racing Rules of Sailing for 2009 – 2012. Dave Perry's 100 Best Racing Rules Quizzes* is published by the United States Sailing Association (US SAILING). For a comprehensive explanation of the rules, read Dave Perry's *Understanding the Racing Rules of Sailing through 2012* which also is available from US SAILING — 1 (800) 877-2451 or www.ussailing.org

ANSWER

Boat W is penalized under rule 11, On the Same Tack, Overlapped. The pre-amble to Section C, At Marks and Obstructions, states that rule 18 does not apply "at a starting mark surrounded by navigable water or at its anchor line from the time the boats are approaching them to start..." Therefore the situation is governed by the rules in Sections A and B. Rule 11 requires W to keep clear of L, which she failed to do. Rule 16.1, Changing Course, requires L to give W room to keep clear when she changes course, which she did. Because L became overlapped to leeward of W from clear astern, rule 17, On the Same Tack; Proper Course, requires L not to sail above her proper course while the boats remain overlapped. However, before the starting signal a boat has no proper course (see definition Proper Course); therefore L is free to sail up to head to wind if she chooses. Because L and W both could have avoided contact, they break rule 14, Avoiding Contact; but neither boat can be penalized for breaking that rule because the contact did not result in damage or injury, and L was the right-of-way boat and W was entitled to room under rule 16.1 [see rule 14(b)].

Answers are based on *The Racing Rules of Sailing for 2009 – 2012. Dave Perry's 100 Best Racing Rules Quizzes* is published by the United States Sailing Association (US SAILING). For a comprehensive explanation of the rules, read Dave Perry's *Understanding the Racing Rules of Sailing through 2012* which also is available from US SAILING — 1 (800) 877-2451 or www.ussailing.org

Quiz 18

Two 25-foot starboard-tack boats, L (a leeward boat) and W (a windward boat), are approaching the right-hand end of the starting line, a 30-foot power-boat, to start an upwind leg. L has come in from clear astern within a length of W. Both boats are sailing close-hauled, with L on a course to pass one boat length to the left of the race committee boat. Ten seconds before the starting signal and when two lengths from the race committee boat, L hails to W, "No room, you're barging!" and luffs slowly to head to wind. W luffs in response and keeps clear. At the starting signal, L makes no effort to bear away despite W's hail to do so. After five seconds W bears away, making slight contact (no damage or injury) with L, and starts. Both boats protest each other. You are on the protest committee; how would you decide this?

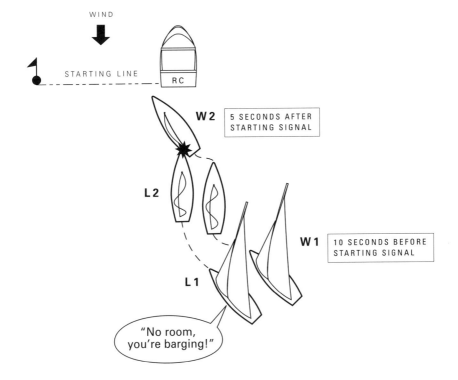

Answers are based on *The Racing Rules of Sailing for 2009 – 2012. Dave Perry's 100 Best Racing Rules Quizzes* is published by the United States Sailing Association (US SAILING). For a comprehensive explanation of the rules, read Dave Perry's *Understanding the Racing Rules of Sailing through 2012* which also is available from US SAILING — 1 (800) 877-2451 or www.ussailing.org

ANSWER

Both boats are penalized. Boat L is penalized for breaking rule 17, On the Same Tack; Proper Course. Because L became overlapped to leeward of W from clear astern, rule 17 requires L not to sail above her proper course while the boats remain overlapped. Before the starting signal, a boat has no proper course (see definition Proper Course); therefore L is free to sail up to head to wind if she chooses. However, at the starting signal, L must sail her proper course, which in this case would be to bear away and fill her sails. By sailing above her proper course after the starting signal, L breaks rule 17. L does not break rule 14, Avoiding Contact, because W changed course so close to L that it was not possible for L to avoid the contact.

Boat W is penalized under rule 11, On the Same Tack, Overlapped, for failing to keep clear of a leeward boat, and rule 14 for failing to avoid contact with L. The fact that L is breaking rule 17 does not compel W to break rules 11 or 14. W is able to keep clear and avoid contact, but fails to do so. Her only recourse against L is to keep clear and protest.

Answers are based on *The Racing Rules of Sailing for 2009 – 2012. Dave Perry's 100 Best Racing Rules Quizzes* is published by the United States Sailing Association (US SAILING). For a comprehensive explanation of the rules, read Dave Perry's *Understanding the Racing Rules of Sailing through 2012* which also is available from US SAILING — 1 (800) 877-2451 or www.ussailing.org

Quiz 19

Boats X and Y are running by the lee, both on port tack. X is five feet clear astern of Y. Suddenly Y swings her boom across and the mainsail fills on her port side. Just before Y's mainsail fills, X luffs sharply and just avoids making contact with Y's transom. X protests Y for gybing too close. You are on the protest committee; how would you decide this?

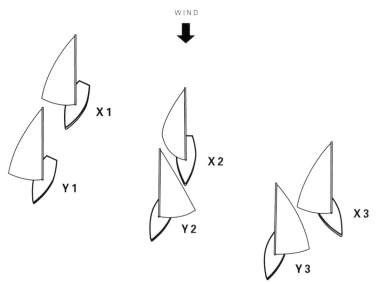

ANSWER

Boat X's protest is disallowed. When both boats are on port tack, Y has the right of way under rule 12, On the Same Tack, Not Overlapped, as the boat clear ahead. When Y gybes and her mainsail lies on her port side, Y has the right-of-way under rule 10, On Opposite Tacks. Rule 15, Acquiring Right of Way, does not apply because Y remains the right-of-way boat throughout, and X is required to keep clear which she did.

Answers are based on *The Racing Rules of Sailing for 2009 – 2012*. *Dave Perry's 100 Best Racing Rules Quizzes* is published by the United States Sailing Association (US SAILING). For a comprehensive explanation of the rules, read Dave Perry's *Understanding the Racing Rules of Sailing through 2012* which also is available from US SAILING — 1 (800) 877-2451 or www.ussailing.org

Quiz 20

Two 30-foot boats, PW (a windward boat) and PL (a leeward boat), are sailing dead downwind on port tack. Boat PL becomes overlapped to leeward of Boat PW from clear astern and the boats are ten feet apart. During the overlap, PW repeatedly reminds PL not to sail above PL's proper course, to which PL responds each time, "I'm sailing my proper course." PW then luffs, moving 30 feet away from PL. PL responds by luffing to within ten feet of PW. PW hails, "Protest!" and flies her protest flag. In the hearing, PL testifies that during the time she was luffing she had been sailing above her proper course, but her luff had not affected PW because PW had voluntarily widened the distance between the two boats. You are on the protest committee; how would you decide this?

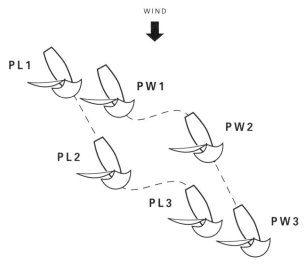

ANSWER

Boat PL is penalized for breaking rule 17, On the Same Tack; Proper Course. Because she became overlapped to leeward from clear astern within two lengths of PW, PL is required to sail no higher than her proper course while she remains overlapped and within two lengths of PW. By sailing above her proper course, PL breaks rule 17.

Answers are based on *The Racing Rules of Sailing for 2009 – 2012*. *Dave Perry's 100 Best Racing Rules Quizzes* is published by the United States Sailing Association (US SAILING). For a comprehensive explanation of the rules, read Dave Perry's *Understanding the Racing Rules of Sailing through 2012* which also is available from US SAILING — 1 (800) 877-2451 or www.ussailing.org

Quiz 21

Boats A (clear ahead) and B (clear astern) are running downwind on starboard tack and are over six lengths from the leeward mark. A is so close to B that, if she were to gybe onto port tack, A could neither cross in front of B nor luff up across B's transom. At no point while the boats are on port tack are the boats overlapped. B continues sailing well past the port-tack layline to the mark, despite A's repeated hails that B is sailing above her proper course and that she must gybe. Finally, A flies her protest flag and B gybes. Both boats approach the leeward mark from well outside the zone on tight reaches. A protests, claiming that B sailed above her proper course when she did not have luffing rights under rule 17, On the Same Tack; Proper Course. You are on the protest committee; how would you decide this?

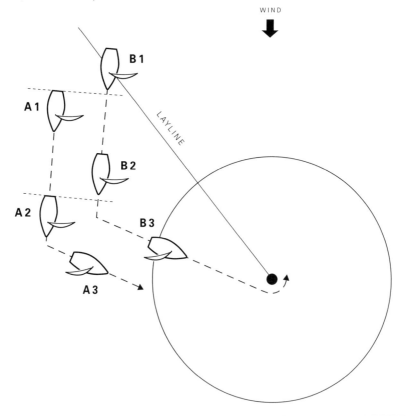

Answers are based on *The Racing Rules of Sailing for 2009 – 2012*. *Dave Perry's 100 Best Racing Rules Quizzes* is published by the United States Sailing Association (US SAILING). For a comprehensive explanation of the rules, read Dave Perry's *Understanding the Racing Rules of Sailing through 2012* which also is available from US SAILING — 1 (800) 877-2451 or www.ussailing.org

ANSWER

Boat A's protest is disallowed. While on starboard tack, A and B are not over-lapped; therefore the proper course limitations in rule 17 do not apply. Rule 12, On the Same Tack, Not Overlapped, requires B, the boat clear astern, to keep clear of A, the boat clear ahead, which she does. In this situation, no other rule limits where B can sail relative to A.

Answers are based on *The Racing Rules of Sailing for 2009 – 2012. Dave Perry's 100 Best Racing Rules Quizzes* is published by the United States Sailing Association (US SAILING). For a comprehensive explanation of the rules, read Dave Perry's *Understanding the Racing Rules of Sailing through 2012* which also is available from US SAILING — 1 (800) 877-2451 or www.ussailing.org

Quiz 22

Two 30-foot boats, W and L, are on a beam reach, with L moving much faster than W. At stage 1, L is approaching W from clear astern and is paralleling W's course about two-and-a-half boat lengths to leeward. At stage 2, still paralleling W's course, L pulls up bow to bow with W. At stage 3, L luffs sharply above her proper course and converges with W. At stage 4, L and W make gentle contact with no damage or injury, and both protest. You are on the protest committee; how would you decide this?

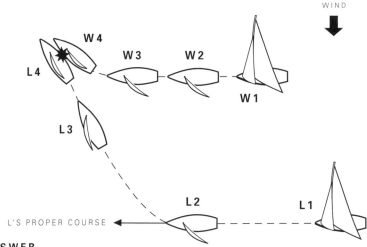

WIND

W 4   W 3   W 2   W 1

L 4   L 3   L 2   L 1

L'S PROPER COURSE

ANSWER

Boat W is penalized under rule 11, On the Same Tack, Overlapped, for failing to keep clear of a leeward boat, and rule 14, Avoiding Contact, for failing to avoid contact when it was possible to do so. Since L does not become overlapped within two lengths of W, the proper course limitation in rule 17, On the Same Tack; Proper Course, doesn't apply. L is free to sail up to head to wind, provided that whenever she changes course she gives W "room to keep clear" under rule 16.1, Changing Course. Regarding the contact, rule 14, Avoiding Contact, requires all boats to avoid contact when reasonably possible. Certainly L could have avoided making contact with W, but didn't; therefore she breaks rule 14. But a right-of-way boat can be penalized under rule 14 only when damage or injury results from the collision [rule 14(b)]. In this case there was neither.

Answers are based on *The Racing Rules of Sailing for 2009 – 2012. Dave Perry's 100 Best Racing Rules Quizzes* is published by the United States Sailing Association (US SAILING). For a comprehensive explanation of the rules, read Dave Perry's *Understanding the Racing Rules of Sailing through 2012* which also is available from US SAILING — 1 (800) 877-2451 or www.ussailing.org

Quiz 23

Boats W (a windward boat) and L (a leeward boat) are reaching towards the gybe mark. L becomes overlapped with W from clear astern. They are both sailing proper courses and are on a collision course. As they near each other, W hails, "You came from clear astern and I'm on my proper course." L replies, "I'm on my proper course." W's boom then touches L with no damage or injury and both protest. You are on the protest committee; how would you decide this?

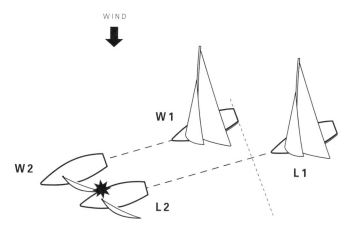

WIND

W 1

W 2

L 1

L 2

ANSWER

Boat W is penalized under rule 11, On the Same Tack, Overlapped, for failing to keep clear of a leeward boat, and rule 14, Avoiding Contact, for failing to avoid contact when it was possible to do so. When L first became overlapped with W, she was required to give W room to keep clear under rule 15, Acquiring Right of Way, which she did. Because L overlaps W from clear astern, rule 17 requires L not to sail above HER proper course. L is sailing on her proper course (not above it) and W fails to keep clear.

L could have avoided making contact with W, but didn't; therefore she breaks rule 14. But a right-of-way boat can be penalized under rule 14 only when damage or injury results from the collision [rule 14(b)]. In this case there was neither.

Answers are based on *The Racing Rules of Sailing for 2009 – 2012. Dave Perry's 100 Best Racing Rules Quizzes* is published by the United States Sailing Association (US SAILING). For a comprehensive explanation of the rules, read Dave Perry's *Understanding the Racing Rules of Sailing through 2012* which also is available from US SAILING — 1 (800) 877-2451 or www.ussailing.org

Quiz 24

Two overlapped boats, W and L, are broad reaching on starboard tack within two lengths of each other. W has caught up with L from clear astern and is attempting to pass her to windward. L begins to slowly luff above her proper course and W keeps clear. When W is within a couple feet of pulling clear ahead, W luffs sharply, clearly breaks the overlap and bears away causing the boats to become overlapped once again. L continues to sail above her proper course in an effort to delay W from passing her. W keeps clear and protests L. You are on the protest committee; how would you decide this?

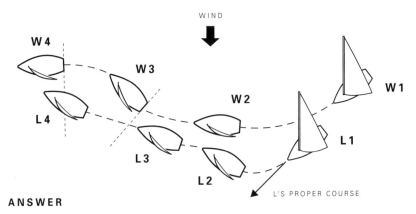

WIND

W 4

W 3

W 2

W 1

L 4

L 3

L 2

L 1

L'S PROPER COURSE

ANSWER

L is penalized under rule 17, On the Same Tack; Proper Course. At positions 1 and 2, W is keeping clear under rules 12, On the Same Tack, Not Overlapped and 11, On the Same Tack, Overlapped, respectively. When L luffs from position 1 to 2, rule 16.1, Changing Course requires her to give W room to keep clear, which she does. At position 3, when W luffs and breaks the overlap, L becomes clear astern of W (see definition Clear Astern and Clear Ahead; Overlap). When W bears away, L becomes overlapped to leeward of W. Rule 17 states, "If a boat clear astern becomes overlapped within two of her hull lengths to leeward of a boat on the same tack, she shall not sail above her proper course…" The fact that it is W's actions that cause the overlap to be broken and then reestablished is immaterial. By sailing above her proper course after she becomes overlapped to leeward of W, L breaks rule 17.

Answers are based on *The Racing Rules of Sailing for 2009 – 2012*. *Dave Perry's 100 Best Racing Rules Quizzes* is published by the United States Sailing Association (US SAILING). For a comprehensive explanation of the rules, read Dave Perry's *Understanding the Racing Rules of Sailing through 2012* which also is available from US SAILING — 1 (800) 877-2451 or www.ussailing.org

Quiz 25

Boats L (a leeward boat) and W (a windward boat) are sailing close-hauled towards the starting line with ten seconds to go before the starting signal. L, with more speed, overlaps W to leeward. As the boats cross the starting line after the gun they are nearly bow to bow. Two lengths later, L luffs up to head to wind. W keeps clear and protests. You are on the protest committee; how would you decide this?

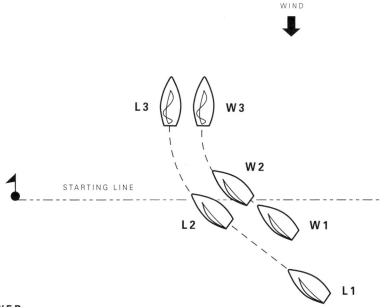

ANSWER

Boat L is penalized for breaking rule 17, On the Same Tack; Proper Course. L becomes overlapped with W from clear astern. Rule 17, therefore, requires her not to sail above her proper course. As a boat has no proper course before her starting signal, L is free to sail up to head to wind if she chooses before the starting signal (see definition Proper Course). But once the starting signal is made, L is required not to sail above her proper course. By sailing head to wind, when there are no factors to indicate that head to wind is L's proper course, L breaks rule 17.

Answers are based on *The Racing Rules of Sailing for 2009 – 2012. Dave Perry's 100 Best Racing Rules Quizzes* is published by the United States Sailing Association (US SAILING). For a comprehensive explanation of the rules, read Dave Perry's *Understanding the Racing Rules of Sailing through 2012* which also is available from US SAILING — 1 (800) 877-2451 or www.ussailing.org

Quiz 26

Two 18-foot boats, L (a leeward boat) and W (a windward boat), are approaching the left-hand end of the starting line, which is a 16-foot powerboat. When W is three lengths from the end of the line, L becomes overlapped on W to leeward from clear astern. There are six seconds to go before the starting signal. L slowly luffs and W keeps clear. As L reaches close-hauled, the starting signal is made. L is a boat length from the powerboat and will not clear it sailing close-hauled. She luffs to head-to-wind, shooting up and around the power-boat, and then bears away to a close-hauled course. W keeps clear throughout, and protests L for sailing above close-hauled after the starting signal. You are on the protest committee: how would you decide this?

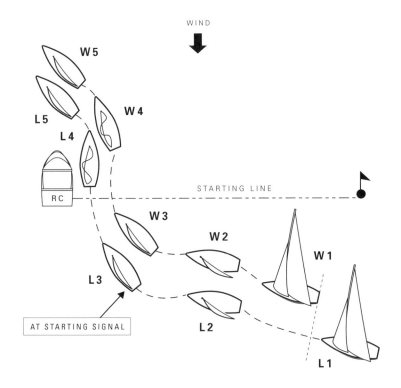

Answers are based on *The Racing Rules of Sailing for 2009 – 2012*. *Dave Perry's 100 Best Racing Rules Quizzes* is published by the United States Sailing Association (US SAILING). For a comprehensive explanation of the rules, read Dave Perry's *Understanding the Racing Rules of Sailing through 2012* which also is available from US SAILING — 1 (800) 877-2451 or www.ussailing.org

ANSWER

Boat W's protest is disallowed. The 16-foot powerboat ranks as both a "mark" and an "obstruction" to the 18-foot boats (see definitions Mark and Obstruction). The preamble to Section C, At Marks and Obstructions, states that rule 18 does not apply "at a starting mark surrounded by navigable water…" Therefore the situation is governed by the rules of Sections A and B. L becomes overlapped to leeward from clear astern of W; therefore, rule 17, On the Same Tack; Proper Course, requires her to not sail above her proper course. Before the starting signal L has no proper course; therefore she is free to sail up to head, provided that when she changes course she gives W room to keep clear (see definition Proper Course and rule 16.1, Changing Course). After the starting signal, L is required to not sail above her proper course. In this case her "proper course" (the course she would sail to finish as soon as possible) is to luff head to wind, coast past the powerboat and then bear away to a close-hauled course (see definition Proper Course). L sails no higher than this course, and therefore does not break rule 17; and while she is changing course, L gives W room to keep clear under rule 16.1 as demonstrated by W's performance. W correctly keeps clear under rule 11, On the Same Tack, Overlapped.

Answers are based on *The Racing Rules of Sailing for 2009 – 2012. Dave Perry's 100 Best Racing Rules Quizzes* is published by the United States Sailing Association (US SAILING). For a comprehensive explanation of the rules, read Dave Perry's *Understanding the Racing Rules of Sailing through 2012* which also is available from US SAILING — 1 (800) 877-2451 or www.ussailing.org

Quiz 27

Two starboard-tack boats, L and W, are approaching the race committee boat marking the right-hand end of the starting line to start. When there are 15 seconds before the starting signal, W overlaps L to windward from clear astern. L luffs and W is able to keep clear. The starting signal is made. With L head to wind, W does not have room to pass between L and the race committee boat. W tells L to bear away immediately to her close-hauled course, but L continues sailing head to wind thereby forcing W onto the wrong side of the race committee boat. L then bears away and starts. W circles around to start and protests L for denying her room at the starting mark by sailing above close-hauled after the starting signal. You are on the protest committee; how would you decide this?

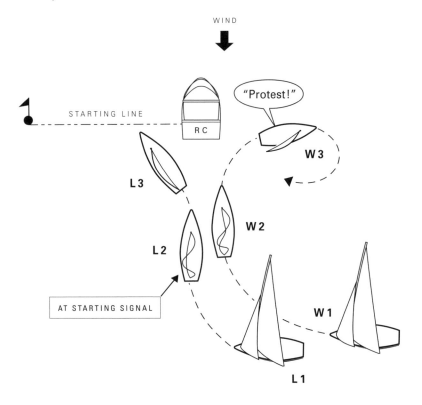

Answers are based on *The Racing Rules of Sailing for 2009 – 2012*. *Dave Perry's 100 Best Racing Rules Quizzes* is published by the United States Sailing Association (US SAILING). For a comprehensive explanation of the rules, read Dave Perry's *Understanding the Racing Rules of Sailing through 2012* which also is available from US SAILING — 1 (800) 877-2451 or www.ussailing.org

ANSWER

Boat W's protest is disallowed. L, as the leeward boat, is the right-of-way boat throughout the incident under rule 11, On the Same Tack, Overlapped. When she luffs (changes course), rule 16.1, Changing Course, requires her to give W room to keep clear, which she clearly does based on W's performance. Before the starting signal, L has no limit on where she can sail; i.e., she is permitted to sail up to head to wind, even when overlapped by just a couple of feet on W.

The only rule that could potentially require L to sail no higher than her proper course after the starting signal is rule 17, On The Same Tack; Proper Course. However, rule 17 only applies when L becomes overlapped to leeward of W from clear astern. As this is not the case, rule 17 does not apply and L breaks no rule by continuing to sail head to wind after the starting signal.

Answers are based on *The Racing Rules of Sailing for 2009 – 2012. Dave Perry's 100 Best Racing Rules Quizzes* is published by the United States Sailing Association (US SAILING). For a comprehensive explanation of the rules, read Dave Perry's *Understanding the Racing Rules of Sailing through 2012* which also is available from US SAILING — 1 (800) 877-2451 or www.ussailing.org

Quiz 28

Boats W (a windward boat) and L (a leeward boat) are sailing close-hauled to-wards the windward mark, with W two lengths to windward of L. For tactical reasons, W wants L to tack, so W bears away 15 degrees below close-hauled, reaches onto L's wind, then luffs back up to close-hauled. L, in bad air, tacks and protests W for sailing below her proper course. You are on the protest commit-tee; how would you decide this?

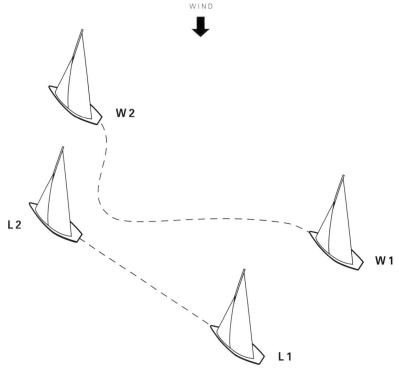

ANSWER

There is no rule requiring W to not sail below her proper course in this situa-tion. W is required to keep clear of L under rule 11, On the Same Tack, Over-lapped, which she does. Boat L's protest is disallowed.

Answers are based on *The Racing Rules of Sailing for 2009 – 2012. Dave Perry's 100 Best Racing Rules Quizzes* is published by the United States Sailing Association (US SAILING). For a comprehensive explanation of the rules, read Dave Perry's *Understanding the Racing Rules of Sailing through 2012* which also is available from US SAILING — 1 (800) 877-2451 or www.ussailing.org

Quiz 29

Boats W and L, two overlapped starboard-tack boats, are sailing on proper courses toward the gybe mark to be rounded to port. When six lengths away from the mark, W bears away approximately 20 degrees in order to slow L, and to try to pull clear ahead before reaching the zone. L protests, claiming that W is sailing below her proper course. W claims that she is sailing on her proper course because by rounding the gybe mark ahead of L she will ultimately finish more quickly. You are on the protest committee; how would you decide this?

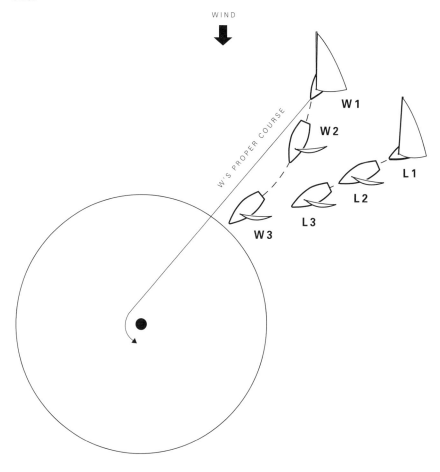

Answers are based on *The Racing Rules of Sailing for 2009 – 2012*. *Dave Perry's 100 Best Racing Rules Quizzes* is published by the United States Sailing Association (US SAILING). For a comprehensive explanation of the rules, read Dave Perry's *Understanding the Racing Rules of Sailing through 2012* which also is available from US SAILING — 1 (800) 877-2451 or www.ussailing.org

ANSWER TO QUIZ 29

There is no rule requiring W to not sail below her proper course in this situation. While the boats are overlapped, W is required to keep clear of L under rule 11, On the Same Tack, Overlapped, which she does. Boat L's protest is disallowed.

Answers are based on *The Racing Rules of Sailing for 2009 – 2012. Dave Perry's 100 Best Racing Rules Quizzes* is published by the United States Sailing Association (US SAILING). For a comprehensive explanation of the rules, read Dave Perry's *Understanding the Racing Rules of Sailing through 2012* which also is available from US SAILING — 1 (800) 877-2451 or www.ussailing.org

Quizzes 30-46

The rules of Part 2, Sections C and D

At Marks and Obstructions and Other Rules

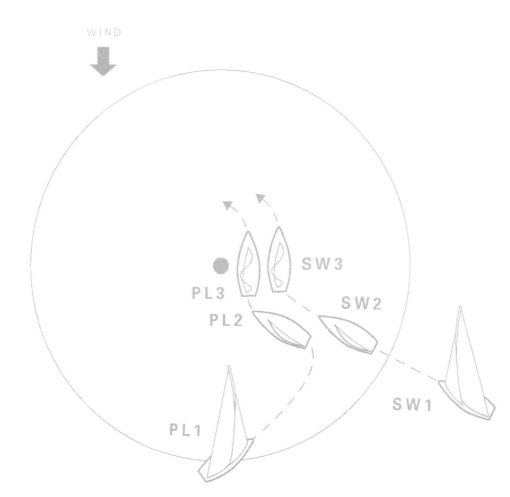

Quiz 30

Boat P (on port tack) is sailing close-hauled within one length of a dock. Boat S (on starboard tack), also close-hauled, is on a collision course with P and hails, "Starboard!" P replies with a hail of "Room to clear the obstruction!" S tacks to avoid the collision and protests. You are on the protest committee; how would you decide this?

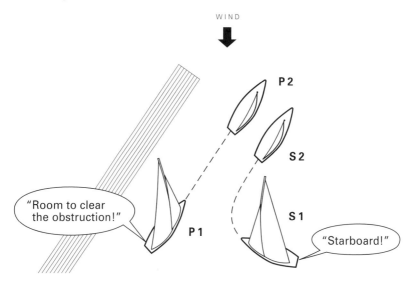

ANSWER

Boat P is penalized under rule 10, On Opposite Tacks. Rule 18.1, When Rule 18 Applies, states that when two boats on opposite tacks are on a beat to windward, rule 18 does not apply between them. Therefore they are subject to rule 10 (a port-tack boat shall keep clear of a starboard-tack boat). Note also that rule 20, Room to Tack at an Obstruction, does not apply because P and S are not on the same tack (see rule 20.1, Hailing and Responding).

Answers are based on *The Racing Rules of Sailing for 2009 – 2012. Dave Perry's 100 Best Racing Rules Quizzes* is published by the United States Sailing Association (US SAILING). For a comprehensive explanation of the rules, read Dave Perry's *Understanding the Racing Rules of Sailing through 2012* which also is available from US SAILING — 1 (800) 877-2451 or www.ussailing.org

Quiz 31

Boats SL and SW, two overlapped boats, are approaching the starting line to start. The right-hand end of the starting line is the end of a breakwater not surrounded by navigable water. As the two boats near the end of the breakwater SL hails SW, "Don't go in there, you're barging." SW replies, "I need room at the obstruction." SL bears away to avoid a collision and protests. You are the protest committee; how would you decide this?

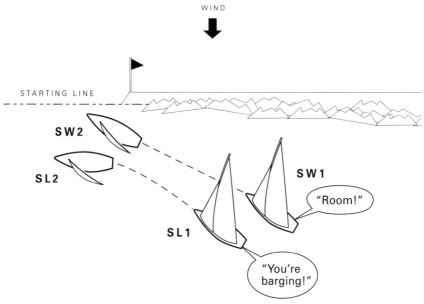

ANSWER

Boat SL's protest is disallowed. The breakwater ranks as both a mark and an obstruction (see definitions Mark and Obstruction). The boats will only be sailing past the end of the obstruction, therefore the obstruction is not a "continuing" obstruction. Because the starting mark is not surrounded by navigable water, the exception in the preamble to Section C does not apply, and rule 18, Mark-Room applies. Specifically, rule 18.2(b), Giving Mark-Room, applies and requires SL to give SW mark-room to pass the end of the breakwater.

Answers are based on *The Racing Rules of Sailing for 2009 – 2012. Dave Perry's 100 Best Racing Rules Quizzes* is published by the United States Sailing Association (US SAILING). For a comprehensive explanation of the rules, read Dave Perry's *Understanding the Racing Rules of Sailing through 2012* which also is available from US SAILING — 1 (800) 877-2451 or www.ussailing.org

Quiz 32

Two 23-foot boats, L (a leeward boat) and W (a windward boat), are approaching the right-hand end of the starting line, a 30-foot powerboat, to start an upwind leg. L is sailing head-to-wind and aiming at the transom of the race committee boat; W is beam reaching on a collision course with L. Ten seconds before the starting signal and when two lengths from the race committee boat, W hails L for room at the obstruction. L replies, "No room!" W quickly luffs and tacks away to avoid hitting L and/or the race committee boat, and protests L for failing to give her room. You are on the protest committee; how would you decide this?

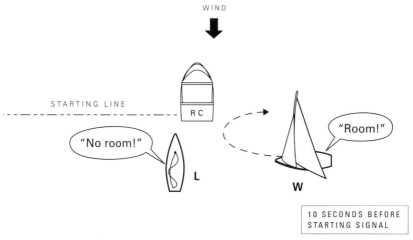

ANSWER

Boat W's protest is disallowed. Though the 30-foot powerboat is an "obstruction" to Boats L and W, it is also a "mark" (see definitions Mark and Obstruction). The preamble to Section C, At Marks and Obstructions, states that rule 18, Mark-Room, does not apply "at a starting mark surrounded by navigable water..." Therefore the situation is governed by the rules of Sections A and B. W correctly keeps clear under rule 11, On the Same Tack, Overlapped.

Answers are based on *The Racing Rules of Sailing for 2009 – 2012. Dave Perry's 100 Best Racing Rules Quizzes* is published by the United States Sailing Association (US SAILING). For a comprehensive explanation of the rules, read Dave Perry's *Understanding the Racing Rules of Sailing through 2012* which also is available from US SAILING — 1 (800) 877-2451 or www.ussailing.org

Quiz 33

Boats W and L are beam reaching along the starting line on starboard tack. Ahead of them, Boat X is nearly motionless on a close-hauled course. To avoid hitting X, W asks L for room to pass to leeward of X. L refuses, claiming that W can pass to windward of X. L passes to leeward of X and W passes to windward of X. W protests L. You are on the protest committee; how would you decide this?

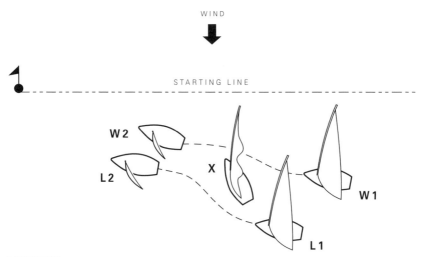

ANSWER

Boat L is penalized for breaking rule 19.2(b), Giving Room at an Obstruction. With respect to X, both L and W are clear astern and therefore required to keep clear of her under rule 12, On the Same Tack, Not Overlapped; X therefore ranks as an obstruction to both (see definition Obstruction). As L and W approach X, L (as the right-of-way boat) has the option of luffing and passing X to windward, or of steering a course to pass X to leeward. When L elects to pass X to leeward, and is overlapped with W, rule 19.2(b) requires her to give room to W, as the inside boat, to do the same. Note that had L elected to luff and pass X to windward, W would be required to keep clear under rule 11, On the Same Tack, Overlapped; and as the outside boat, to give room under rule 19.2(b).

Answers are based on *The Racing Rules of Sailing for 2009 – 2012*. Dave Perry's *100 Best Racing Rules Quizzes* is published by the United States Sailing Association (US SAILING). For a comprehensive explanation of the rules, read Dave Perry's *Understanding the Racing Rules of Sailing through 2012* which also is available from US SAILING — 1 (800) 877-2451 or www.ussailing.org

Quiz 34

Boats S (a 32-foot starboard-tack boat) and P (a 36-foot port-tack boat) are approaching the starting line for a downwind start at one end of the starting line which is marked by a 50-foot powerboat. The compass course to the first mark is dead downwind. The boats are each broad reaching, and are on a course to collide right at the starting mark, with P on the inside. When the boats are two lengths from the mark, the starting signal is made. P hails S for room and S replies, "No room at a starting mark – Starboard!" S then bears away to avoid a collision, and protests P under rule 10, On Opposite Tacks. You are on the protest committee; how would you decide this?

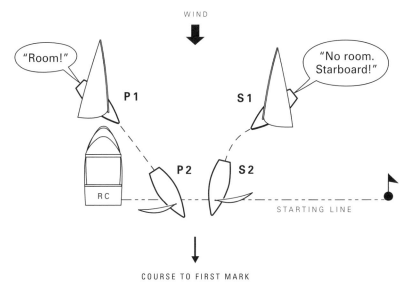

ANSWER

Boat P is penalized for breaking rule 10, On Opposite Tacks. The 50-foot power-boat ranks as both a "mark" and an "obstruction" (see definitions Mark and Obstruction). The preamble to Section C, At Marks and Obstructions, states that rule 18, Mark-Room, does not apply "at a starting mark surrounded by navigable water…" Therefore the situation is governed by the rules in Sections A and B. By not keeping clear of S, P breaks rule 10.

Answers are based on *The Racing Rules of Sailing for 2009 – 2012. Dave Perry's 100 Best Racing Rules Quizzes* is published by the United States Sailing Association (US SAILING). For a comprehensive explanation of the rules, read Dave Perry's *Understanding the Racing Rules of Sailing through 2012* which also is available from US SAILING — 1 (800) 877-2451 or www.ussailing.org

Quiz 35

Boat S (on starboard tack) is approaching the leeward mark to be rounded to starboard. Boat P (on port tack) is similarly approaching the leeward mark on a collision course with S. When three lengths from the mark, P hails "Mark-room" to S. S remains silent. When right at the mark, P begins to gybe inside of S and S is forced to bear away to avoid hitting P. S protests P. You are on the protest committee; how would you decide this?

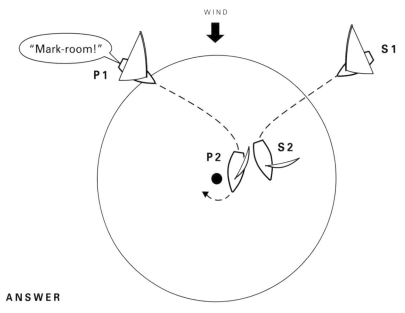

ANSWER

Boat S's protest is disallowed; neither boat is penalized. Rule 18.2(b), Mark-Room: Giving Mark-Room, applies because the two boats are in the zone (within three lengths of the mark; see definition Zone). Though on opposite tacks, S and P are considered "overlapped" because they both are sailing below 90 degrees to the true wind, and because rule 18, Mark-Room, applies to them (see the definition Overlap). S, as the outside boat, is required to give P, the inside boat, mark-room, which includes space to gybe when it is a normal part of the rounding maneuver (see definition Mark-Room). S complies with rule 18.2(b) and P does not take more room than S is required to provide.

Answers are based on *The Racing Rules of Sailing for 2009 – 2012. Dave Perry's 100 Best Racing Rules Quizzes* is published by the United States Sailing Association (US SAILING). For a comprehensive explanation of the rules, read Dave Perry's *Understanding the Racing Rules of Sailing through 2012* which also is available from US SAILING — 1 (800) 877-2451 or www.ussailing.org

Quiz 36

Boats A and B are approaching the leeward mark broad reaching on starboard tack. When A reaches the zone, B is clear astern. Prior to gybing to round the mark, A slows down and B becomes overlapped to windward of A. A swings wide of the mark to prepare to make a tactical "swing wide-cut close" rounding; i.e., sail her proper course around the mark. When she gybes, her boom strikes B's port shroud with no damage or injury. B protests, claiming that A took more room than she is entitled to. You are on the protest committee; how would you decide this?

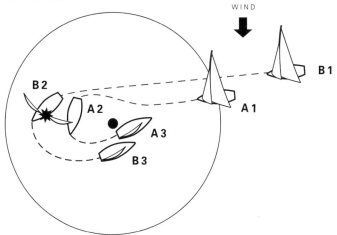

ANSWER

Boat B is penalized under rule 18.2(b), Mark-Room: Giving Mark-Room. When A reaches the zone (see definition Zone), B is clear astern of her at that time, and is therefore required by rule 18.2(b) to give A mark-room (see definition Mark-Room). When B becomes overlapped with A she must continue to give A mark-room as well as keep clear of her under rule 11, On the Same Tack, Overlapped. When the boats become overlapped, rule 18.4, Mark-Room: Gybing, requires A (the right-of-way boat) not to sail farther from the mark before gybing than needed to sail her proper course; A did not do so. Though A breaks rule 14, Avoiding Contact, by not avoiding contact with B when it was reasonably possible for her to do so, she was entitled to mark-room and there is no damage or injury; therefore she cannot be penalized under rule 14 [see rule 14(b)].

Answers are based on *The Racing Rules of Sailing for 2009 – 2012. Dave Perry's 100 Best Racing Rules Quizzes* is published by the United States Sailing Association (US SAILING). For a comprehensive explanation of the rules, read Dave Perry's *Understanding the Racing Rules of Sailing through 2012* which also is available from US SAILING — 1 (800) 877-2451 or www.ussailing.org

Quiz 37

A port-tack boat (PL) and a starboard-tack boat (SW) are approaching the windward mark. When less than three lengths from the mark, PL tacks to leeward of SW. During the tack, SW does not have to take action to avoid contact with PL. After the tack, the two boats sail for one length at which point PL luffs head to wind to make it around the mark. To keep clear of PL, SW luffs head to wind also and there is no contact. SW protests PL. You are on the protest committee; how would you decide this?

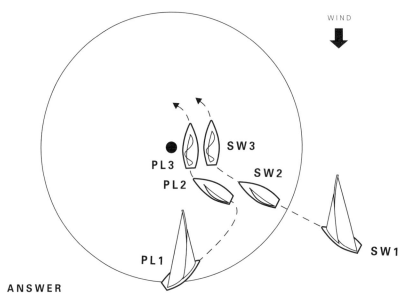

ANSWER

Boat PL is penalized under rule 18.3(a), Mark-Room: Tacking When Approaching a Mark. Rule 18.3(a) states, "If two boats were approaching a mark on opposite tacks and one of them changes tack, and as a result is subject to rule 13 in the zone when the other is fetching the mark…the boat that changed tack …shall not cause the other boat to sail above close-hauled to avoid her…" Rule 18, Mark-Room, applies until both boats have left the zone; therefore rule 18.3(a) continues to apply when PL luffs to make the mark. PL completes her tack within the zone, and when she luffs to make the mark she causes SW to sail above close-hauled to avoid her, thereby breaking rule 18.3(a).

Answers are based on *The Racing Rules of Sailing for 2009 – 2012*. *Dave Perry's 100 Best Racing Rules Quizzes* is published by the United States Sailing Association (US SAILING). For a comprehensive explanation of the rules, read Dave Perry's *Understanding the Racing Rules of Sailing through 2012* which also is available from US SAILING — 1 (800) 877-2451 or www.ussailing.org

Quiz 38

A port-tack boat (PA) and a starboard-tack boat (SB) are approaching the windward mark. PA tacks to pass the mark, and completes her tack (i.e., arrives at a close-hauled course) within the zone. At that moment she is one length ahead and slightly to windward of SB, and moving more slowly than SB due to her tack. SB holds her course. As PA begins to bear away around the mark it becomes apparent that SB will hit PA's leeward side, and that there will not be room for SB to sail between PA and the mark without hitting either. PA luffs away from the mark and SB passes between PA and the mark with no contact. PA protests SB. You are on the protest committee; how would you decide this?

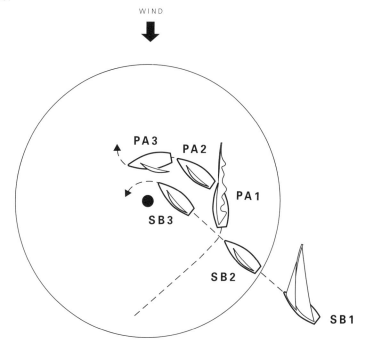

WIND

ANSWER TO QUIZ 38

PA's protest is disallowed; neither boat broke a rule. When PA completes her tack within the zone, she does not cause SB to sail above close-hauled to avoid her, nor does she prevent her from passing the mark. Therefore PA does not break rule 18.3(a), Mark-Room: Tacking When Approaching a Mark. Rule 18.3(b) requires PA to keep clear of SB if SB becomes overlapped inside her at any time while the boats are passing the mark. By keeping clear of SB, PA complies with rule 18.3(b) and rule 11, On the Same Tack, Overlapped.

Answers are based on *The Racing Rules of Sailing for 2009 – 2012. Dave Perry's 100 Best Racing Rules Quizzes* is published by the United States Sailing Association (US SAILING). For a comprehensive explanation of the rules, read Dave Perry's *Understanding the Racing Rules of Sailing through 2012* which also is available from US SAILING — 1 (800) 877-2451 or www.ussailing.org

Quiz 39

Within one hull length of a windward mark to be left to port, Boat PL (an 18-foot boat on port tack) tacks to a close-hauled course to leeward of Boat SW (on starboard tack). As PL's bow approaches the mark, SW remains close-hauled and hails to PL, "You have no rights!" As SW bears away to round the mark she forces PL to bear away into the mark to avoid hitting her. PL immediately gets clear of the other boats, hailing "Protest!" as she does, and does one turn that includes a tack and a gybe. SW sails on. After the race, PL files her protest against SW for failing to keep clear of her. You are on the protest committee; how would you decide this?

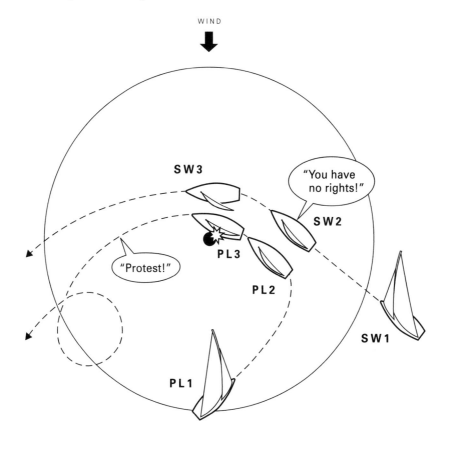

Answers are based on *The Racing Rules of Sailing for 2009 – 2012. Dave Perry's 100 Best Racing Rules Quizzes* is published by the United States Sailing Association (US SAILING). For a comprehensive explanation of the rules, read Dave Perry's *Understanding the Racing Rules of Sailing through 2012* which also is available from US SAILING — 1 (800) 877-2451 or www.ussailing.org

ANSWER TO QUIZ 39

Boat SW is penalized under rule 11, On the Same Tack, Overlapped. As PL approaches SW on the opposite tack, PL is required to keep clear under rule 10, On Opposite Tacks. Once PL is on a close-hauled course, she becomes the right-of-way boat (as the leeward boat), and is required by rule 15, Acquiring Right of Way, to initially give SW room to keep clear of her. Throughout the maneuver, PL never needs to take avoiding action; therefore SW keeps clear and gives room as required.

When PL completes her tack within the zone at the mark, rule 18.3(a), Mark-Room: Tacking When Approaching a Mark, requires that she not cause SW to sail above close-hauled to avoid her or prevent SW from passing the mark. She did neither; therefore she did not break rule 18.3(a). Once PL is on a close-hauled course and overlapped to leeward of SW, SW (as the windward boat) becomes required to keep clear of her under rule 11. By bearing away towards PL and causing PL to take action to avoid her, SW breaks rule 11. PL chooses to take a penalty for touching the mark. This, however, does not remove her right to also protest SW. Based on the facts, SW breaks rule 11 and is penalized. The fact that PL took a One-Turn Penalty cannot be undone. However, had PL not taken a penalty, she would be exonerated by the protest committee for breaking rule 31, Touching a Mark, under rule 64.1(c), Penalties and Exoneration.

Answers are based on *The Racing Rules of Sailing for 2009 – 2012*. *Dave Perry's 100 Best Racing Rules Quizzes* is published by the United States Sailing Association (US SAILING). For a comprehensive explanation of the rules, read Dave Perry's *Understanding the Racing Rules of Sailing through 2012* which also is available from US SAILING — 1 (800) 877-2451 or www.ussailing.org

Quiz 40

At an upwind finish, two close-hauled boats on opposite tacks (S and P) are converging at the left end mark of the finishing line. When about a length and a half from the mark, P completes a tack to leeward of S without fouling her. However, in order to pass the mark on the correct side, P luffs up to almost head to wind, thereby causing S to sail above close-hauled to avoid her. P beats S across the line. S protests P. You are on the protest committee; how would you decide this?

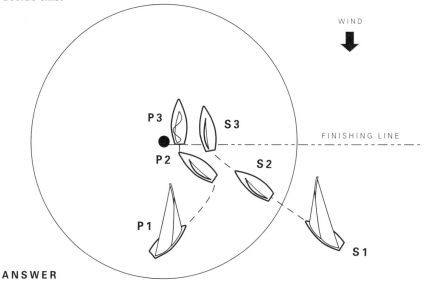

ANSWER

Boat P is penalized for breaking rule 18.3(a), Mark-Room: Tacking When Approaching a Mark. As P and S are approaching the finishing mark on opposite tacks, rule 18, Mark-Room, does not apply because the boats are on opposite tacks on a beat to windward; but once P tacks, the boats are no longer on opposite tacks and rule 18 begins to apply (see rule 18.1, When Rule 18 Applies). When a boat has approached another boat on the opposite tack and has then completed a tack within the zone at a mark, rule 18.3(a) requires the boat that tacked to not cause the other boat to have to sail above close-hauled to avoid her. P causes S to sail above close-hauled to avoid her; therefore she breaks rule 18.3(a).

Answers are based on *The Racing Rules of Sailing for 2009 – 2012. Dave Perry's 100 Best Racing Rules Quizzes* is published by the United States Sailing Association (US SAILING). For a comprehensive explanation of the rules, read Dave Perry's *Understanding the Racing Rules of Sailing through 2012* which also is available from US SAILING — 1 (800) 877-2451 or www.ussailing.org

Quiz 41

In a fleet race, two boats (LI and WO) are sailing down the first reach of a triangle course and are about to round the gybe mark. In order to sail her proper course LI must gybe at the mark. WO had come up from clear astern of LI and had overlapped her to windward when the boats were about ten lengths from the mark. The boats remain overlapped as they enter the zone. Rather than sail her proper course and gybe at the mark, LI decides to delay WO slightly by continuing on past the mark without gybing. When three lengths past the mark, LI gybes. WO gybes also and protests LI. You are on the protest committee; how would you decide this?

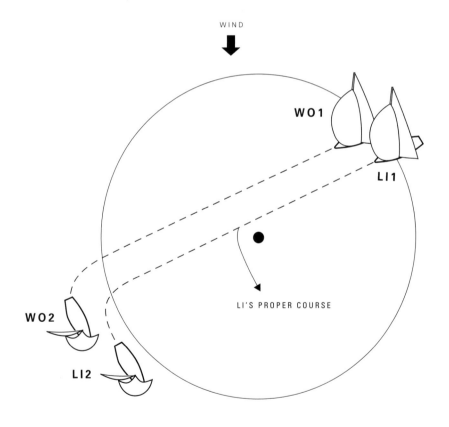

Answers are based on *The Racing Rules of Sailing for 2009 – 2012*. *Dave Perry's 100 Best Racing Rules Quizzes* is published by the United States Sailing Association (US SAILING). For a comprehensive explanation of the rules, read Dave Perry's *Understanding the Racing Rules of Sailing through 2012* which also is available from US SAILING — 1 (800) 877-2451 or www.ussailing.org

ANSWER TO QUIZ 41

Boat LI is penalized under rule 18.4, Mark-Room: Gybing. LI's proper course (i.e., her fastest course to the finish line) is to gybe at the mark. LI is both the right-of-way boat (as the leeward boat) and the inside boat, and she is overlapped with WO when she is in the zone. Because LI's proper course includes a gybe at the mark, rule 18.4 requires her to sail no farther from the mark than is necessary to sail her proper course until she gybes. However, LI continues on past the mark for three lengths before gybing, therefore breaking rule 18.4.

NOTE: If this scenario had occurred at a gate mark or in a team race, the answer would be different; i.e., the protest would be disallowed. The reason is that rule 18.4 does not apply at a gate mark (see rule 18.4), and the Team Racing Appendix deletes rule 18.4 [rule D1.1(c)]. Therefore, because LI did not establish the overlap from clear astern of WO, the requirement for LI to sail her proper course under rule 17, On the Same Tack; Proper Course, does not apply; and because rule 18.4 does not apply at a gate mark or in team racing, there is no requirement for LI to gybe and sail her proper course at the mark.

Answers are based on *The Racing Rules of Sailing for 2009 – 2012. Dave Perry's 100 Best Racing Rules Quizzes* is published by the United States Sailing Association (US SAILING). For a comprehensive explanation of the rules, read Dave Perry's *Understanding the Racing Rules of Sailing through 2012* which also is available from US SAILING — 1 (800) 877-2451 or www.ussailing.org

Quiz 42

Boats SW and SL, two starboard-tack boats, are sailing close-hauled nearby each other heading for a breakwater. SL, the leeward boat, hails SW for room to tack. SW, the windward boat, replies, "You tack." SL immediately tacks but has to bear away substantially to pass astern of SW without colliding with her. She does so and protests SW claiming SW did not give her enough room as demonstrated by her need to bear away substantially to avoid SW. You are on the protest committee; how would you decide this?

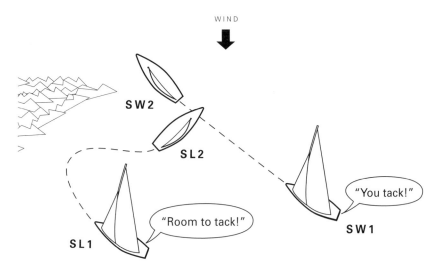

ANSWER

Boat SL's protest is disallowed. By her actions SL demonstrates that she is able to tack immediately and avoid SW. Thus SW has complied with rule 20.1(b), Hailing and Responding. Nothing in rule 20 is intended to protect the hailing boat from a loss of distance incurred by bearing away astern of the hailed boat. Once on port tack, SL properly avoids SW under rule 10, On Opposite Tacks. (See ISAF Case 35.)

Answers are based on *The Racing Rules of Sailing for 2009 – 2012*. Dave Perry's *100 Best Racing Rules Quizzes* is published by the United States Sailing Association (US SAILING). For a comprehensive explanation of the rules, read Dave Perry's *Understanding the Racing Rules of Sailing through 2012* which also is available from US SAILING — 1 (800) 877-2451 or www.ussailing.org

Quiz 43

Boats PW and PL, two close-hauled port-tack boats, are half a length apart and approaching Boat S, a close-hauled starboard-tack boat. If PL and S hold their courses PL will hit S amidships. PW hails PL for room to pass astern of S. PL then hails PW for room to tack at S. PW does not respond and begins bearing away to pass astern of S. PL bears away also to avoid a collision and protests PW. In the hearing PW defends her actions by saying that she hailed first. You are on the protest committee; how would you decide this?

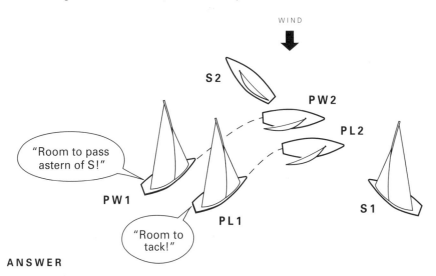

ANSWER

Boat PW is penalized for breaking rule 20.1(b), Room to Tack at an Obstruction; Hailing and Responding. S is an obstruction to PL and PW because they both need to keep clear of S (see definition Obstruction). Rule 19.2(b), Giving Room at an Obstruction, does not apply because the preamble to Section C states that when rule 20 applies, rule 19 does not. Rule 20 applies because safety requires the leeward boat (PL) to make a substantial course change to avoid an obstruction (S) and PL intends to tack. It is immaterial which boat hails first. Rule 20.1 specifically permits PL to hail PW for room to tack at the obstruction; and requires PW to respond in one of two ways (either tack or reply "You tack"). PW does neither and thereby breaks rule 20.1(b). (See US SAILING Appeal 24.)

Answers are based on *The Racing Rules of Sailing for 2009 – 2012. Dave Perry's 100 Best Racing Rules Quizzes* is published by the United States Sailing Association (US SAILING). For a comprehensive explanation of the rules, read Dave Perry's *Understanding the Racing Rules of Sailing through 2012* which also is available from US SAILING — 1 (800) 877-2451 or www.ussailing.org

Quiz 44

Boats PA and PB, two port-tack boats, are beam reaching parallel to the starting line with PA half a length clear ahead of PB. PA is on a collision course with the midships part of a starboard tacker up ahead. PA realizes she can't tack without fouling PB. In this scenario, does PA have the right to hail PB for room to tack at the starboard tacker?

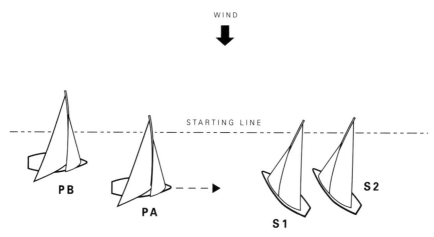

ANSWER

No. Rule 20.1, Room to Tack at an Obstruction, is available to PA only when she is on a close-hauled course or above. In this case she is beam reaching. Note that PB does not need to be on a close-hauled course in order to be hailed; it is only PA that must be close-hauled or above.

Answers are based on *The Racing Rules of Sailing for 2009 – 2012*. *Dave Perry's 100 Best Racing Rules Quizzes* is published by the United States Sailing Association (US SAILING). For a comprehensive explanation of the rules, read Dave Perry's *Understanding the Racing Rules of Sailing through 2012* which also is available from US SAILING — 1 (800) 877-2451 or www.ussailing.org

Quiz 45

After the starting signal, Boats L and W are heading towards the anchor line of the race committee boat that marks the left end of the starting line. Both L and W have started, i.e., crossed the starting line, but neither can clear the anchor line without tacking. L hails W for room to tack, but W holds her course. L luffs her sails to avoid hitting the anchor line, and W tacks away. L protests W. You are on the protest committee; how would you decide this?

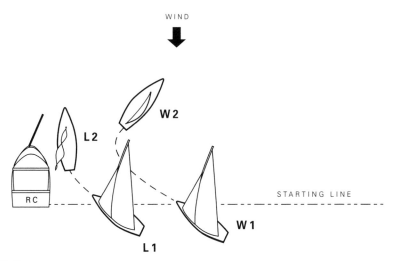

ANSWER

Boat L's protest is disallowed. The race committee boat's anchor line requires the boats to make substantial alterations of course to avoid it; therefore the anchor line ranks as an obstruction. Rule 20.1, Room to Tack at an Obstruction (a Section C rule) permits a leeward close-hauled boat to hail for room to tack at an obstruction. However, the preamble to Section C states, "The rules in Section C do not apply at a starting mark surrounded by navigable water or at its anchor line from the time boats are approaching them to start until they have passed them…" The race committee boat is a starting mark; and because L and W have not passed its anchor line yet, rule 20 does not apply. Therefore W is not required to respond to L's hail, nor give L room to tack.

Answers are based on *The Racing Rules of Sailing for 2009 – 2012*. Dave Perry's *100 Best Racing Rules Quizzes* is published by the United States Sailing Association (US SAILING). For a comprehensive explanation of the rules, read Dave Perry's *Understanding the Racing Rules of Sailing through 2012* which also is available from US SAILING — 1 (800) 877-2451 or www.ussailing.org

Quiz 46

Immediately after the starting signal, the race committee signals an 'Individual Recall' and clearly hails Boat S's number. S (on starboard tack) luffs her sails in an attempt to slow down so she can clear herself from other boats and return to start. Boat P (on port tack), on a collision course with S, decides that S is a "premature starter" with no rights, and tries to cross ahead of S. S bears away ten degrees to avoid P, and protests. You are on the protest committee; how would you decide this?

ANSWER

Boat P is penalized under rule 10, On Opposite Tacks. Under rule 21.1, Starting Errors; Taking Penalties; Moving Astern, S does not lose her right of way until she is sailing back towards the pre-start side of the starting line or its extensions.

Answers are based on *The Racing Rules of Sailing for 2009 – 2012. Dave Perry's 100 Best Racing Rules Quizzes* is published by the United States Sailing Association (US SAILING). For a comprehensive explanation of the rules, read Dave Perry's *Understanding the Racing Rules of Sailing through 2012* which also is available from US SAILING — 1 (800) 877-2451 or www.ussailing.org

Quizzes 47-51

The rules of Part 3

Conduct of a Race

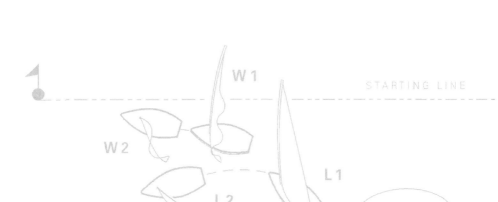

Quiz 47

Five seconds prior to the start, Boat M is reaching along the starting line awaiting the starting gun so she can luff to close-hauled and start the race. Five to eight seconds later, and still no starting gun, some boats luff to close-hauled and start. Ten seconds later the gun sounds and M starts. She finishes poorly in the race and requests redress under rule 62.1(a), Redress. At the hearing the race committee chairman explains that the class flag was lowered precisely at the correct time but the shotgun misfired several times until it finally went off ten seconds late. You are on the protest committee; how would you decide this?

ANSWER

Boat M's request for redress is denied. Rule 26, Starting Races, states that "Times shall be taken from the visual signals; the absence of a sound signal shall be disregarded."

Answers are based on *The Racing Rules of Sailing for 2009 – 2012*. *Dave Perry's 100 Best Racing Rules Quizzes* is published by the United States Sailing Association (US SAILING). For a comprehensive explanation of the rules, read Dave Perry's *Understanding the Racing Rules of Sailing through 2012* which also is available from US SAILING — 1 (800) 877-2451 or www.ussailing.org

Quiz 48

Immediately before the starting signal, the crew on Boat X hikes out and momentarily extends his arms straight out over his head. At the starting signal his hands are on the course side of the starting line but the boat's hull is behind the line. The race committee signals an individual recall, and subsequently scores X as OCS (On the Course Side) because she did not return to the pre-start side of the line and start thereby breaking rule 28.1, Sailing the Course. X requests redress under rule 62.1(a), Redress. At the hearing, X claims that the race committee has erred in that her hull was behind the starting line at the starting signal, and her crew's hands were not in a normal position at the time. You are on the protest committee; how would you decide this?

ANSWER

The race committee's action to score Boat X OCS is upheld. Rule 28.1, Sailing the Course, requires boats to "start." The definition Start states that "A boat starts when, having been entirely on the pre-start side of the starting line at or after her starting signal, and having complied with rule 30.1 if it applies, any part of her hull, crew or equipment crosses the starting line in the direction of the first mark." No mention is made of "normal position." Because X did not have her hull, crew and equipment entirely on the pre-start side of the line at or after the starting signal, she failed to start. Under rule A5, Scores Determined by the Race Committee, the race committee has the authority to score X OCS without giving her a hearing.

Answers are based on *The Racing Rules of Sailing for 2009 – 2012*. *Dave Perry's 100 Best Racing Rules Quizzes* is published by the United States Sailing Association (US SAILING). For a comprehensive explanation of the rules, read Dave Perry's *Understanding the Racing Rules of Sailing through 2012* which also is available from US SAILING — 1 (800) 877-2451 or www.ussailing.org

Quiz 49

After a general recall, the fleet is preparing to start again. At the preparatory signal, the crew of Boat X look for, but see no, flag "I" displayed on the race committee boat. At 30 seconds to go before the start, X is over the line, but immediately dips back and is entirely behind the line at the starting signal. X finishes third in the race but is scored OCS (On the Course Side) by the race committee who believes that rule 30.1, I Flag Rule, is automatically in effect after a general recall. The sailing instructions make no amendments to rule 30.1. X requests redress under rule 62.1(a), Redress. You are on the protest committee; how would you decide this?

ANSWER

Boat X started correctly and is reinstated in the race and given her score for her third place finish. Rule 30.1 only applies when flag "I" is properly displayed, unless the sailing instructions modify the rule which in this case they did not. To put rule 30.1 into effect, the race committee must display flag "I" as the preparatory signal (see rule 26, Starting Races and Race Signals). The race committee did not display flag "I" in this case; therefore rule 30.1 is not in effect.

Answers are based on *The Racing Rules of Sailing for 2009 – 2012. Dave Perry's 100 Best Racing Rules Quizzes* is published by the United States Sailing Association (US SAILING). For a comprehensive explanation of the rules, read Dave Perry's *Understanding the Racing Rules of Sailing through 2012* which also is available from US SAILING — 1 (800) 877-2451 or www.ussailing.org

Quiz 50

Boat Q is beating towards the finishing line in very light winds and adverse current. Just after her bow crosses the finishing line, she bears away and sails off the course. Boat P protests Q for failing to completely cross the finishing line. You are on the protest committee; how would you decide this?

ANSWER

Boat P's protest is disallowed; Boat Q is scored in her finishing position. Boat Q "finished" when her bow crossed the finishing line (see definition Finishing). Rule 28.1, Sailing the Course, states, "After finishing she need not cross the finishing line completely."

Answers are based on *The Racing Rules of Sailing for 2009 – 2012*. *Dave Perry's 100 Best Racing Rules Quizzes* is published by the United States Sailing Association (US SAILING). For a comprehensive explanation of the rules, read Dave Perry's *Understanding the Racing Rules of Sailing through 2012* which also is available from US SAILING — 1 (800) 877-2451 or www.ussailing.org

Quiz 51

The sailing instructions state that the time limit for the race is two hours. Boat X misunderstands the race course and fails to round the last mark. She finishes in 1 hour and 45 minutes. Boat Y crosses the finishing line next in 2:10, followed by the rest of the fleet. Boat Z, who finishes ninth, protests Boat X for failing to sail the course correctly and thereby breaking rule 28.1, Sailing the Course. The protest committee disqualifies Boat X for failing to sail the course correctly. The race committee, deciding that the race is valid because Boat X finished within the time limit, posts the scores of the boats as they crossed the finishing line. Boat Z requests redress under rule 62.1(a), Redress, claiming the race should be abandoned. You are on the protest committee; how would you decide this?

ANSWER

The race is abandoned. Rule 35, Time Limit and Scores, states, " If one boat sails the course as required in rule 28.1 and finishes within the time, if any, all boats that finish shall be scored... If no boat finishes within the time limit, the race committee shall abandon the race." Boat X was protested and found by the protest committee to have not sailed the course as required in rule 28.1. The next boat to finish (Boat Y) did not do so within the two-hour time limit. Therefore the race is abandoned.

Answers are based on *The Racing Rules of Sailing for 2009 – 2012. Dave Perry's 100 Best Racing Rules Quizzes* is published by the United States Sailing Association (US SAILING). For a comprehensive explanation of the rules, read Dave Perry's *Understanding the Racing Rules of Sailing through 2012* which also is available from US SAILING — 1 (800) 877-2451 or www.ussailing.org

Quizzes 52-69

The rules of Part 4

Other Requirements
When Racing

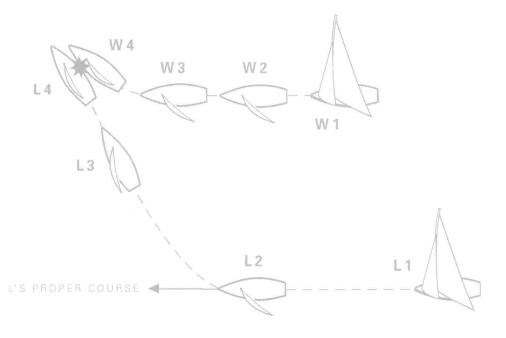

Quiz 52

During a race, a Laser sailor wears hiking pants with stiffeners under his thighs. He is protested for breaking rule 49.1, Crew Position. You are on the protest committee; how would you decide this?

ANSWER

Protest disallowed. Rule 49.1 states, "Competitors shall use no device designed to position their bodies outboard, other than hiking straps and stiffeners worn under the thighs." Therefore, wearing stiffeners under the thighs does not break rule 49.1.

Answers are based on *The Racing Rules of Sailing for 2009 – 2012. Dave Perry's 100 Best Racing Rules Quizzes* is published by the United States Sailing Association (US SAILING). For a comprehensive explanation of the rules, read Dave Perry's *Understanding the Racing Rules of Sailing through 2012* which also is available from US SAILING — 1 (800) 877-2451 or www.ussailing.org

Quiz 53

Boats A and B are drifting toward a downwind finish in very light wind with A directly ahead of B. Suddenly B does a large roll-gybe followed immediately by a second one. As she completes each of her gybes, B is clearly moving faster than A, a boat in the same class experiencing the same wind that has not gybed. The speed generated by the two roll-gybes is enough to move her just ahead of A. A protests B. In her defense, B claims that her gybes were a tactical move to position herself into a passing lane, and that rule 42.2(e), Propulsion, permits tacks and gybes for tactical purposes. You are on the protest committee, how would you decide this?

ANSWER

Boat B is penalized for breaking rule 42.1, Propulsion, because her actions of rolling the boat in her two consecutive gybes increase her speed beyond that generated by the natural action of the wind and water. Rule 42.3(b) permits a boat to roll-tack or roll-gybe provided the boat's speed immediately after the tack or gybe is not greater than it was immediately before. Rule 42.2(e) simply prohibits all repeated tacks and gybes that are unrelated to tactical considerations; it does not permit tactical tacks and gybes that otherwise infringe rule 42.1.

Answers are based on *The Racing Rules of Sailing for 2009 – 2012*. *Dave Perry's 100 Best Racing Rules Quizzes* is published by the United States Sailing Association (US SAILING). For a comprehensive explanation of the rules, read Dave Perry's *Understanding the Racing Rules of Sailing through 2012* which is also available from US SAILING — 1 (800) 877-2451 or www.ussailing.org

Quiz 54

Very near to the finish line in adverse current and light air, Boat Q's crew tosses her anchor out in front of the boat such that the anchor crosses the finishing line before landing in the water. After the anchor is well set in the bottom, Q's crew raises the anchor in such a way that the boat is pulled over the finishing line in the process. Deeming that anchoring is a normal maneuver in sailboat racing fully allowed under the rules, and realizing that the rules require the retrieval of the anchor, the race committee scores the boat in her finishing place. Boat B protests Boat Q. You are on the protest committee; how would you decide this?

ANSWER

Boat Q is penalized for breaking rule 42.1, Propulsion. Rule 45, Hauling Out; Making Fast; Anchoring, permits a boat to anchor provided the anchor is recovered before continuing in the race. However, by raising the anchor in such a way that she propels herself past the point she is at when she lowers her anchor, Q illegally propels herself and breaks rule 42.1. (See ISAF Case 5.)

NOTE: When the anchor in mid-air crosses the finish line, Boat Q has not yet finished because the anchor is not in "normal position" (see definition Finish).

Answers are based on *The Racing Rules of Sailing for 2009 – 2012. Dave Perry's 100 Best Racing Rules Quizzes* is published by the United States Sailing Association (US SAILING). For a comprehensive explanation of the rules, read Dave Perry's *Understanding the Racing Rules of Sailing through 2012* which also is available from US SAILING — 1 (800) 877-2451 or www.ussailing.org

Quiz 55

Boat X is approaching a downwind finishing line in very light air. There is a strong current moving across the race course. Just before finishing, X is swept by the current onto the anchor line of the race committee boat marking one end of the finish line. By holding onto the line for about fifteen seconds, the crew of X keeps her from touching the committee boat and a slight puff of wind fills in enabling X to gain forward speed and finish. Boat Y protests X for touching the mark. You are on the protest committee; how would you decide this?

ANSWER

Boat X is penalized under rule 42.1, Propulsion, and rule 45, Hauling Out; Making Fast; Anchoring; she is not penalized under rule 31, Touching a Mark. The anchor line of a mark is not part of the mark itself (see definition Mark). There is no penalty for touching the anchor line of a mark. However, rule 42.1 states, "...a boat shall compete by using only the wind and water to increase, maintain or decrease her speed." By holding onto the anchor line of the committee boat, X breaks rule 42.1. Rule 45 prohibits a boat from being made fast by means other than anchoring or standing on the bottom. Though X is protested under rule 31, rule 64.1(a), Penalties and Exoneration, requires that a boat found to have broken a rule be penalized irrespective of whether the rule that led to the penalization was mentioned in the protest.

Answers are based on *The Racing Rules of Sailing for 2009 – 2012*. *Dave Perry's 100 Best Racing Rules Quizzes* is published by the United States Sailing Association (US SAILING). For a comprehensive explanation of the rules, read Dave Perry's *Understanding the Racing Rules of Sailing through 2012* which also is available from US SAILING — 1 (800) 877-2451 or www.ussailing.org

Quiz 56

In 18 knots of breeze, Laser X is about 10 seconds early for the start, so her helmsman leans back and drags his upper body in the water for 5 seconds, effectively slowing the boat and permitting a proper start. Having witnessed this, a competitor protests Laser X. You are on the protest committee; how would you decide this?

ANSWER

Laser X is penalized for breaking rule 42.1, Propulsion, which states, "…a boat shall compete by using only the wind and water to increase, maintain or decrease her speed." The helmsman of Laser X used the dragging of his upper body to slow the boat, which breaks rule 42.1.

Answers are based on *The Racing Rules of Sailing for 2009 – 2012. Dave Perry's 100 Best Racing Rules Quizzes* is published by the United States Sailing Association (US SAILING). For a comprehensive explanation of the rules, read Dave Perry's *Understanding the Racing Rules of Sailing through 2012* which also is available from US SAILING — 1 (800) 877-2451 or www.ussailing.org

Quiz 57

Given that you are sailing a dinghy and that there are no modifications to rule 42, Propulsion, in effect, how would you answer the following questions:

1) How many "pumps" per wave are allowed to initiate surfing downwind?

2) How much "ooching" per wave is allowed to initiate surfing downwind?

3) Is roll-tacking and/or roll-gybing permitted?

ANSWER

The answers to all three questions are contained in rules 42.2, Propulsion: Prohibited Actions, and 42.3, Propulsion: Exceptions.

1) "Pumping" is defined by rule 42.2(a) as "repeated fanning of any sail..." However rule 42.3(c) permits one "pull" of the sheet and / or guy controlling any sail; i.e., the mainsheet and/or the spinnaker sheet and/or the spinnaker guy can each be pulled once per wave. Note that there is no restriction on which part(s) of the mainsheet can be held while pumping.

2) None. "Ooching" is prohibited at all times [rule 42.2(c)].

3) Yes, both are allowed, provided the "roll" doesn't make the boat go faster after the tack or gybe than it was going immediately prior to the tack or gybe [rules 42.3(a) and (b)]. However, repeated tacks or gybes unrelated to changes in the wind or to tactical considerations break rule 42.2(e) even if they do not make the boat go faster.

Answers are based on *The Racing Rules of Sailing for 2009 – 2012*. *Dave Perry's 100 Best Racing Rules Quizzes* is published by the United States Sailing Association (US SAILING). For a comprehensive explanation of the rules, read Dave Perry's *Understanding the Racing Rules of Sailing through 2012* which also is available from US SAILING — 1 (800) 877-2451 or www.ussailing.org

Quiz 58

Boat A is approaching a port-hand windward mark in very light air, close-hauled on starboard tack. Because she is not quite making the mark, her helmsman puts the tiller to leeward but the boat does not turn enough to miss the mark. In order to turn faster, the helmsman returns the tiller approximately to amidships and forcefully pushes it to leeward several times, being careful to never let the tiller cross the boat's centerline. She clears the mark by about two feet. Now above close-hauled, and to continue turning around the mark, the helmsman pulls the tiller to windward and returns it to approximately amidships several times forcefully in order to turn the boat back down to close-hauled. Boat B protests A for these actions. You are on the protest committee; how would you decide this?

ANSWER

Boat A is penalized for breaking rule 42.2(d), Propulsion: Prohibited Actions, which says that repeated movement of the helm that is forceful is sculling. In turning to windward from a close-hauled course by repeatedly moving her helm forcefully, Boat A is sculling, which is prohibited by rule 42.2(d). The facts that her actions are necessary for steering and that she is not propelling the boat are immaterial. However, rule 42.3(d), Propulsion: Exceptions, permits a boat that is above close-hauled and stationary or moving slowly to scull to turn to a close-hauled course. Therefore A breaks rule 42.2(d) when she is sculling to turn to windward to avoid the mark, but not while she is sculling to turn back down to a close-hauled course.

Answers are based on *The Racing Rules of Sailing for 2009 – 2012*. *Dave Perry's 100 Best Racing Rules Quizzes* is published by the United States Sailing Association (US SAILING). For a comprehensive explanation of the rules, read Dave Perry's *Understanding the Racing Rules of Sailing through 2012* which also is available from US SAILING — 1 (800) 877-2451 or www.ussailing.org

Quiz 59

In a fleet race in two knots of wind, Boat Y powers under engine into the starting area shortly before the preparatory signal at a speed of 5 knots. At the preparatory signal she is moving at the same rate of speed with her engine running but out of gear. At two-and-a-half minutes before the starting signal she raises her sails, and slows to one-and-three-quarter knots. Boat X protests her for breaking rule 42.1, Propulsion. You are on the protest committee; how would you decide this?

ANSWER

Boat X's protest is disallowed. Y begins "racing" at her preparatory signal (see definition Racing). During the period in which Y is racing she is not propelled by anything other than the wind and the water. The fact that her speed after the preparatory signal is greater than the wind alone would have provided, is the result of her momentum created by engine power that propelled her before she began racing. Nothing in the rules requires that a boat be in any particular state of motion or non-motion when she begins racing. Therefore rule 42.1 is not broken. (See ISAF Case 69.)

   NOTE: In match racing, rule 42 also applies between the warning and preparatory signals, so a boat cannot be propelled by her engine after her warning signal (see rule C2.10).

Answers are based on *The Racing Rules of Sailing for 2009 – 2012. Dave Perry's 100 Best Racing Rules Quizzes* is published by the United States Sailing Association (US SAILING). For a comprehensive explanation of the rules, read Dave Perry's *Understanding the Racing Rules of Sailing through 2012* which also is available from US SAILING — 1 (800) 877-2451 or www.ussailing.org

Quiz 60

Shortly after gybing around a reaching mark, Boat Z's crew accidentally falls overboard. During the time it takes the helmsman to lower the spinnaker and turn back to recover his crew, Boat T picks the crew up and returns him to Z. The crew is not injured. With her crew back aboard she continues in the race and finishes, but is protested under rule 41, Outside Help, for receiving outside help. You are on the protest committee; how would you decide this?

ANSWER

Boat Z is penalized for breaking rule 41, Outside Help. Though rule 1.1, Safety: Helping Those in Danger, requires that every boat give all possible help to any person or vessel in danger, rule 41 makes no specific exception for receiving outside help unless the crew is ill or injured.

Answers are based on *The Racing Rules of Sailing for 2009 – 2012. Dave Perry's 100 Best Racing Rules Quizzes* is published by the United States Sailing Association (US SAILING). For a comprehensive explanation of the rules, read Dave Perry's *Understanding the Racing Rules of Sailing through 2012* which also is available from US SAILING — 1 (800) 877-2451 or www.ussailing.org

Quiz 61

On a chilly, light-air day, the helmsman of Boat Z, a dinghy, is protested for wearing clothing in excess of that allowed by rule 43.1(b), Competitor Clothing and Equipment. The applicable class rules and sailing instructions do not make any rulings with regard to the wearing of clothing. There is no dispute over the fact that the clothes were intended for warmth and not for the purpose of increasing weight, and that the clothes remained relatively dry during the race. The clothing, when weighed in compliance with Appendix H, Weighing Clothing and Equipment, weighs 22 pounds (10 kilograms). This does not include the helmsman's boots or socks. The helmsman argues that (a) the weight is immaterial because the clothes were not intended or used to increase his weight, and (b) that 22 pounds (10 kilograms) is within the legal weight parameter. You are on the protest committee; how would you decide this?

ANSWER

Boat Z is penalized for breaking rule 43.1(b). The maximum weight allowed by rule 43.1(b) is 8 kilograms (18 pounds) unless the class rules or the sailing instructions specify a higher weight, in which case the maximum they can prescribe is 10 kilograms (22 pounds). In this case, no prescriptions to this rule are made. Rule 43.1(a) prohibits competitors from wearing clothing or equipment for the purpose of increasing their weight. Because Boat Z's helmsman was wearing the clothing solely for warmth, so he did not break rule 43.1(a). However, because the weight of his clothing exceeded the 18 pound limit, he broke rule 43.1(b).

Answers are based on *The Racing Rules of Sailing for 2009 – 2012. Dave Perry's 100 Best Racing Rules Quizzes* is published by the United States Sailing Association (US SAILING). For a comprehensive explanation of the rules, read Dave Perry's *Understanding the Racing Rules of Sailing through 2012* which also is available from US SAILING — 1 (800) 877-2451 or www.ussailing.org

Quiz 62

Two close-hauled boats on a beat (S and P) are on a collision course. When a couple of lengths away from S, P begins bearing away to pass astern of S. S holds her course. Just as it appears to S that P is about to pass astern, P misjudges her course and collides with S, doing considerable damage to the aft port corner of S's hull and stern pulpit. S protests P and P immediately takes a Two-Turns Penalty. S, after stopping to make some repairs, manages to finish the race though she is unable to proceed at full speed due to the damage. She loses several places as a result. Ashore, S files her protest against P and also requests redress. You are on the protest committee; how would you decide this?

ANSWER

Boat P is penalized under rules 10, On Opposite Tacks, 14, Avoiding Contact, and 44.1, Penalties at the Time of an Incident; and S is granted redress under rule 64.2, Decisions on Redress. By colliding with S, P fails to keep clear of S thereby breaking rule 10; and fails to avoid a collision thereby breaking rule 14. Furthermore, the collision causes serious damage to S. Therefore P is required by rule 44.1 to retire; i.e., the Two-Turns Penalty is not available when the rules breach causes serious damage. Because P does not retire, she breaks rule 44.1.

Clearly, S could not have reasonably avoided this collision; therefore she does not break rule 14. And because S's finishing place in the race is made significantly worse by the physical damage caused by P, a boat that was breaking a rule of Part 2, and because the collision occurs through no fault of her own, S is entitled to redress under rule 62.1(b), Redress.

Answers are based on *The Racing Rules of Sailing for 2009 – 2012*. *Dave Perry's 100 Best Racing Rules Quizzes* is published by the United States Sailing Association (US SAILING). For a comprehensive explanation of the rules, read Dave Perry's *Understanding the Racing Rules of Sailing through 2012* which also is available from US SAILING — 1 (800) 877-2451 or www.ussailing.org

Quiz 63

Boat S (on starboard tack) is close-hauled and Boat P (on port tack) is broad reaching on a course taking her clear of S. When they are approximately two lengths apart, a gust strikes S and she rounds up out of control and collides with P. P immediately hails "Protest," flies her protest flag, and does a Two-Turns Penalty. In her protest she claims that S is at fault by breaking rule 16.1, Changing Course. S challenges P's right to protest given that P did a Two-Turns Penalty immediately after the incident. You are on the protest committee; how would you decide this?

ANSWER

Boat P's protest is valid and is to be heard. Rule 63.1, Hearings: Requirement for a Hearing, states that the protest committee shall hear all protests that have been delivered to the race office. If the protest committee finds in favor of S, then P can receive no further penalty (see rule 64.1(b), Penalties and Exoneration). If, however, the protest committee finds in favor of P, then S is penalized under rule 64.1(a), Penalties and Exoneration, for breaking rule 16.1.

Answers are based on *The Racing Rules of Sailing for 2009 – 2012*. *Dave Perry's 100 Best Racing Rules Quizzes* is published by the United States Sailing Association (US SAILING). For a comprehensive explanation of the rules, read Dave Perry's *Understanding the Racing Rules of Sailing through 2012* which also is available from US SAILING — 1 (800) 877-2451 or www.ussailing.org

Quiz 64

With one minute to go before the starting signal, Boat P (on port tack) tries to tack in to leeward of Boat S (on starboard tack). During the tack, S luffs to avoid contact and protests P. P immediately gets clear of S and takes a Two-Turns Penalty before the starting signal has sounded. P gets a good start and crosses S shortly thereafter. S protests P for not doing her Two-Turns Penalty after the starting signal. You are on the protest committee; how would you decide this?

ANSWER

Boat S's protest is disallowed. Boat P has complied with rule 44.2, One-Turn and Two-Turns Penalties. There is no requirement that a boat breaking a rule before the start take her penalty after the starting signal, nor that she take her penalty behind the starting line. Rule 44.2 simply requires that the boat gets well clear of other boats as soon after the incident as possible and promptly takes her penalty.

Answers are based on *The Racing Rules of Sailing for 2009 – 2012. Dave Perry's 100 Best Racing Rules Quizzes* is published by the United States Sailing Association (US SAILING). For a comprehensive explanation of the rules, read Dave Perry's *Understanding the Racing Rules of Sailing through 2012* which also is available from US SAILING — 1 (800) 877-2451 or www.ussailing.org

Quiz 65

Boat Q touches the windward mark. Instead of bearing away around the mark, Q continues on a close-hauled course for a length or so, and when well clear of the other boats she promptly tacks and then gybes and continues in the race. Boat T protests her for not doing a 360 degree turn after touching the mark. You are on the protest committee; how would you decide this?

ANSWER

Boat T's protest is disallowed. Rules 44.1 and 44.2, Penalties at the Time of an Incident, permit a boat that has touched a mark to take a One-Turn Penalty by getting well clear of other boats as soon as possible and then promptly making one turn that includes a tack and a gybe. Boat Q properly complies with rule 44.2 and is therefore exonerated for touching the mark.

Answers are based on *The Racing Rules of Sailing for 2009 – 2012*. *Dave Perry's 100 Best Racing Rules Quizzes* is published by the United States Sailing Association (US SAILING). For a comprehensive explanation of the rules, read Dave Perry's *Understanding the Racing Rules of Sailing through 2012* which also is available from US SAILING — 1 (800) 877-2451 or www.ussailing.org

Quiz 66

During a race, Boats X and Y, two 30-foot boats, are involved in an incident. The Scoring Penalty (20%) described in rule 44.3, Scoring Penalty, is in effect. X hails "Protest" but does not fly a red flag. Y flies a yellow flag immediately after the incident. Two legs later, X sees Y removing her yellow flag just before finishing. X immediately flies her red flag and hails "Protest" again. Y finishes with no flag flying, and makes no report to the race committee. X protests. You are on the protest committee; how would you decide this?

ANSWER

Boat Y is disqualified from the race for breaking rule 44.3(b), Scoring Penalty, which requires a boat that has displayed a yellow penalty flag to keep it displayed until she has finished, as well as calling the race committee's attention to her flag at the finishing line and identifying to the race committee the other boat involved in the incident. Boat X's protest in the first incident was not valid because she failed to fly a red flag as required by rule 61.1(a), Informing the Protestee. However her protest for Y's removal of the yellow flag is valid because she flew her red flag and hailed "Protest" immediately upon seeing its removal.

Answers are based on *The Racing Rules of Sailing for 2009 – 2012. Dave Perry's 100 Best Racing Rules Quizzes* is published by the United States Sailing Association (US SAILING). For a comprehensive explanation of the rules, read Dave Perry's *Understanding the Racing Rules of Sailing through 2012* which also is available from US SAILING — 1 (800) 877-2451 or www.ussailing.org

Quiz 67

SCENARIO 1:

Boat X rounds the windward mark to begin the run. As she bears away, with no spinnaker pole set, her crew begins to hoist the spinnaker. As the spinnaker nears full hoist, X gybes, and the crew fills the spinnaker. X sails for one minute before attempting to put the spinnaker pole up. Has X broken any rule by her "gybe-set"?

SCENARIO 2:

Boat X is sailing down the run. Suddenly her spinnaker pole breaks. The crew lowers it to the deck, and during the three minutes it takes to repair the pole the crew keeps the spinnaker full with no pole attached whatsoever. Has X broken any rule by sailing down the leg with the spinnaker set and drawing and no spinnaker pole attached?

SCENARIO 3:

X approaches the leeward mark with her spinnaker set. When about two minutes away, her crew lowers the pole and stows it on the deck, thereafter keeping the spinnaker full for at least one more minute. X then bears away to round the mark, lowers the spinnaker as the boat gybes, and luffs up onto a close-hauled course by the mark. Has X broken any rule by her "floater-drop"?

ANSWER

In all three scenarios, Boat X has broken no rule. Rule 50, Setting and Sheeting Sails, does not require the use of a spinnaker pole at any time. Therefore, X's maneuvers break no rule.

Answers are based on *The Racing Rules of Sailing for 2009 – 2012. Dave Perry's 100 Best Racing Rules Quizzes* is published by the United States Sailing Association (US SAILING). For a comprehensive explanation of the rules, read Dave Perry's *Understanding the Racing Rules of Sailing through 2012* which also is available from US SAILING — 1 (800) 877-2451 or www.ussailing.org

Quiz 68

Two boats, L and W are approaching the race committee boat to start. L hails, "Don't go in there, you're barging" to W. Nevertheless, W unsuccessfully tries to squeeze between L and the committee boat, and hits both in the process with no damage or injury. She immediately gets clear, takes a Two-Turns Penalty and starts. L protests, claiming that in addition to fouling her, W also hit the mark (the committee boat) and failed to do a penalty turn for that foul. You are on the protest committee; how would you decide this?

ANSWER

Neither boat is penalized. Rule 44.1(a), Taking a Penalty, states that when a boat may have broken a rule in Part 2 and in the same incident has touched a mark, she need not take the penalty for touching the mark, which is a One-Turn Penalty.

Regarding the contact, it was reasonably possible for both boats to have avoided the contact; therefore both boats broke rule 14, Avoiding Contact. However, W took a penalty so cannot be further penalized for breaking rule 14 (see rule 64.1(b), Penalties and Exoneration). And S, as the right-of-way boat, cannot be penalized for breaking rule 14 as the contact did not result in any damage or injury.

Answers are based on *The Racing Rules of Sailing for 2009 – 2012. Dave Perry's 100 Best Racing Rules Quizzes* is published by the United States Sailing Association (US SAILING). For a comprehensive explanation of the rules, read Dave Perry's *Understanding the Racing Rules of Sailing through 2012* which also is available from US SAILING — 1 (800) 877-2451 or www.ussailing.org

Quiz 69

Boat X rounds the windward mark to begin the run. She immediately sets her spinnaker but for several minutes the tack of the spinnaker is at least two feet from the outboard end of the pole. Has X broken any rule?

ANSWER

No, Boat X breaks no rule. Rule 50, Setting and Sheeting Sails, does not require that the tack of the spinnaker be in close proximity to the outboard end of the spinnaker pole when the pole is in use.

Answers are based on *The Racing Rules of Sailing for 2009 – 2012. Dave Perry's 100 Best Racing Rules Quizzes* is published by the United States Sailing Association (US SAILING). For a comprehensive explanation of the rules, read Dave Perry's *Understanding the Racing Rules of Sailing through 2012* which also is available from US SAILING — 1 (800) 877-2451 or www.ussailing.org

Quizzes 70-88

The rules of Part 5, Part 7 and the Appendices

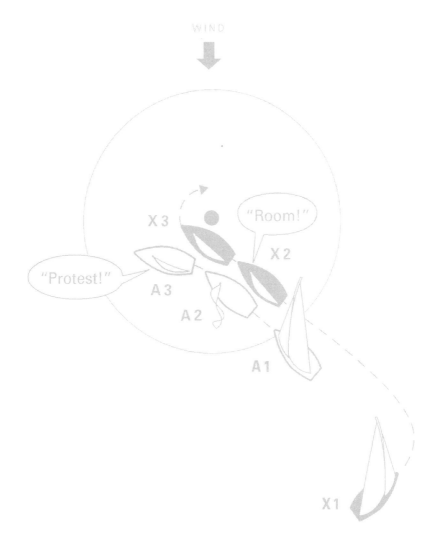

Quiz 70

Boat S (on starboard tack) bears away to avoid hitting Boat P (on port tack) and intends to protest. S immediately shouts out P's name and displays her protest flag, notifies P ashore that a protest will be filed and delivers her protest within the time limit. At the hearing, in response to questioning from the protest committee, S states that she did not hail the actual word "Protest" because she was confident that P was fully aware that she intended to protest. You are on the protest committee; how would you decide this?

ANSWER

Under rule 63.5, Hearings: Validity of the Protest or Request for Redress, the hearing is closed because S's protest is not valid. Rule 61.1(a), Protest Requirements: Informing the Protestee, requires S to hail "Protest." S does not do this. Rule 63.5 requires that at the beginning of the hearing the protest committee decide whether all the requirements for the protest have been met. If not, the hearing must be closed.

Answers are based on *The Racing Rules of Sailing for 2009 – 2012. Dave Perry's 100 Best Racing Rules Quizzes* is published by the United States Sailing Association (US SAILING). For a comprehensive explanation of the rules, read Dave Perry's *Understanding the Racing Rules of Sailing through 2012* which also is available from US SAILING — 1 (800) 877-2451 or www.ussailing.org

Quiz 71

Shortly before finishing, Boats PW (a windward boat) and PL (a leeward boat) are sailing close-hauled on port tack. As they approach the finishing line, PW hails PL for room to pass astern of Boat S (on starboard tack). PL passes astern of S and finishes. PW, believing she was not given sufficient room, tacks onto starboard tack to leeward of S, gybes onto port tack, luffs up to a close-hauled course, tacks to starboard tack once again to finish, then hails "Protest" to PL. At the hearing, PL claims the hail was not made "at the first reasonable opportunity." You are on the protest committee; how would you decide this?

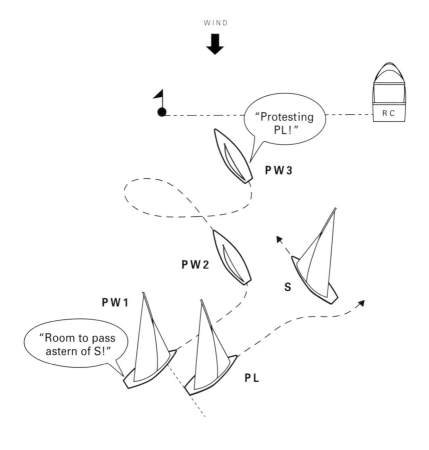

Answers are based on *The Racing Rules of Sailing for 2009 – 2012*. *Dave Perry's 100 Best Racing Rules Quizzes* is published by the United States Sailing Association (US SAILING). For a comprehensive explanation of the rules, read Dave Perry's *Understanding the Racing Rules of Sailing through 2012* which also is available from US SAILING — 1 (800) 877-2451 or www.ussailing.org

ANSWER

Under rule 63.5, Hearings: Validity of the Protest or Request for Redress, the hearing is closed because S's protest is not valid. Rule 61.1(a), Protest Requirements: Informing the Protestee, requires S to hail "Protest" at the first reasonable opportunity after the incident. "First reasonable opportunity" means as soon as practicable, not as soon as convenient. The maneuvers performed by PW after the incident and before hailing clearly demonstrate that her hail is not made at the first reasonable opportunity. Rule 63.5 requires that at the beginning of the hearing the protest committee decide whether all the requirements for the protest have been met. If not, the hearing must be closed. (See US SAILING Appeal 61.)

Answers are based on *The Racing Rules of Sailing for 2009–2012. Dave Perry's 100 Best Racing Rules Quizzes* is published by the United States Sailing Association (US SAILING). For a comprehensive explanation of the rules, read Dave Perry's *Understanding the Racing Rules of Sailing through 2012* which also is available from US SAILING — 1 (800) 877-2451 or www.ussailing.org

Quiz 72

True or False? In order to lodge a valid protest, the protesting boat must display a red flag (as opposed to any other color flag), providing no modifications to rule 61.1(a), Protest Requirements: Informing the Protestee, have been made in the sailing instructions, and provided the boat's hull length is 6 meters or longer.

ANSWER

True. Rule 61.1(a) states, "A boat intending to protest because of an incident occurring in the racing area…shall conspicuously display a red flag at the first reasonable opportunity…" The only two exceptions are when the hull length of the protesting boat is less than 6 meters, and if the incident results in damage or injury that is obvious to the boats involved [see rules 61.1(a)(2) and (3)].

Answers are based on *The Racing Rules of Sailing for 2009 – 2012*. *Dave Perry's 100 Best Racing Rules Quizzes* is published by the United States Sailing Association (US SAILING). For a comprehensive explanation of the rules, read Dave Perry's *Understanding the Racing Rules of Sailing through 2012* which also is available from US SAILING — 1 (800) 877-2451 or www.ussailing.org

Quiz 73

Boats X and Y, two 30-foot boats, are rounding the windward mark in 18 knots of breeze, with X just behind Y. While setting her spinnaker X loses sight of Y and collides with her transom, bending X's bow pulpit and Y's stern pulpit and doing other obvious damage to both boats. Both boats yell "Protest" and continue setting their spinnakers. Neither boat flies a protest flag. After finishing, Y sails by X and says she is protesting her for the collision, and Y properly files the written protest on shore. You are on the protest committee; will you hear this protest?

ANSWER

Yes. Boat Y's protest is valid. Because the incident resulted in damage that was obvious to both boats, neither boat was required to say "Protest" or fly a protest flag. See rule 61.1(a)(3), Protest Requirements: Informing the Protestee. Rule 61.1(a) requires Y to inform X of her intention to protest at the first reasonable opportunity, which she does.

Answers are based on *The Racing Rules of Sailing for 2009 – 2012. Dave Perry's 100 Best Racing Rules Quizzes* is published by the United States Sailing Association (US SAILING). For a comprehensive explanation of the rules, read Dave Perry's *Understanding the Racing Rules of Sailing through 2012* which also is available from US SAILING — 1 (800) 877-2451 or www.ussailing.org

Quiz 74

During a race, the race committee observes Boats A and B go around a mark the wrong way. The race committee does not give them a horn as they finish and scores them "Did not finish" for not sailing the course properly. The boats request redress under rule 62.1(a), Redress, claiming that they did in fact finish properly. You are on the protest committee; how would you decide this?

ANSWER

Boats A and B are reinstated in the race to their finishing places under rule 64.2, Decisions on Redress. Rule 63.1, Hearings: Requirement for a Hearing, states, "A boat...shall not be penalized without a hearing..." except in some situations that do not apply in this case. The race committee has the authority, under rule A5, Scores Determined by the Race Committee, to score a boat "Did not finish" without a hearing only when that boat fails to "finish," i.e., cross the finishing line correctly (see the definition Finish). A and B finish in the defined meaning of the word, and therefore the race committee has no authority to penalize them without a hearing.

   In this case, the race committee observes A and B sail the course incorrectly, i.e., apparently break rule 28.1, Sailing the Course. If they want to act against these boats, they must protest them under rule 60.2(a), Right to Protest; Right to Request Redress or Rule 69 Action, which will initiate a hearing by the protest committee.

Answers are based on *The Racing Rules of Sailing for 2009 – 2012*. *Dave Perry's 100 Best Racing Rules Quizzes* is published by the United States Sailing Association (US SAILING). For a comprehensive explanation of the rules, read Dave Perry's *Understanding the Racing Rules of Sailing through 2012* which also is available from US SAILING — 1 (800) 877-2451 or www.ussailing.org

Quiz 75

One minute after the preparatory signal, the race committee moves one of the starting marks upwind about 30 feet. No boat flies a flag at that time. After the finish, Boat Z, who finishes in tenth place, requests redress under rule 62.1(a), Redress. At the redress hearing, Z claims that even though her start was not affected, the race committee committed an error. She cites rule 27.2, Other Race Committee Actions Before the Starting Signal, which states, "No later than the preparatory signal, the race committee may move a starting mark..." She requests that the race be abandoned, citing rule 64.2, Decisions on Redress. You are on the protest committee; how would you decide this?

ANSWER

Boat Z's request for redress is denied. A boat that claims that her score in a race has been made significantly worse through no fault of her own by an improper action of the race committee can request redress from the protest committee under rule 62.1(a). A protest flag need not be displayed (see rule 62.2).

Consideration of a request for redress under rule 62 involves three questions: 1) Did the race committee make an improper action? 2) If so, was the score of the boat significantly worsened by the improper action through no fault of the boat itself? And 3) if so, what action can be taken by way of compensation for the affected boat or boats that will be as equitable as possible to all competitors? In this case, Z testified at the hearing that her start had not been affected by the moving of the starting mark, but argued that the movement was clearly not permitted under the rules. Although the race committee made an improper action, Z's finishing place, i.e., her score in the race, was not worsened by the action.

Answers are based on *The Racing Rules of Sailing for 2009 – 2012. Dave Perry's 100 Best Racing Rules Quizzes* is published by the United States Sailing Association (US SAILING). For a comprehensive explanation of the rules, read Dave Perry's *Understanding the Racing Rules of Sailing through 2012* which also is available from US SAILING — 1 (800) 877-2451 or www.ussailing.org

Quiz 76

In the first race of a two-race day, Boat B finishes first and gets a gun as she crosses the finishing line. In the second race, she calculates that she need only finish better than 6th place to win the series. She finishes 4th. Ashore she looks at the posted results and finds herself in second place overall, with an OCS (On the Course Side of the Starting Line) listed for race 1. She requests redress claiming that the race committee's improper action of giving her a gun as she crossed the finishing line in race 1 misled her into developing a flawed strategy in race 2. You are on the protest committee; how would you decide this?

ANSWER

No redress should be granted. Unless specifically stated in the sailing instructions, sound signals made or not made by the race committee to signify when boats cross a finishing line have no significance because they are not defined by the rules. Therefore, Boat B must assume the responsibility for her error in relying on such a signal.

Answers are based on *The Racing Rules of Sailing for 2009 – 2012. Dave Perry's 100 Best Racing Rules Quizzes* is published by the United States Sailing Association (US SAILING). For a comprehensive explanation of the rules, read Dave Perry's *Understanding the Racing Rules of Sailing through 2012* which also is available from US SAILING — 1 (800) 877-2451 or www.ussailing.org

Quiz 77

Boats P (on port tack) and S (on starboard tack), intending to race, are sailing about in the racing area 15 minutes before their starting signal. Accidentally P collides with S, putting a large hole in S's topside. S hails "Protest" and flies her protest flag immediately and sails back to shore. Once ashore, S files a protest against P under rule 10, On Opposite Tacks, and a request for redress under rule 62.1(b), Redress. You are on the protest committee; how would you decide this?

ANSWER

Boat S is granted redress under rule 64.2, Decisions on Redress; no penalty is given to Boat P. The preamble to Part 2 states in part, "The rules of Part 2 apply between boats that are sailing in or near the racing area and intend to race..." Therefore, Part 2 of *The Racing Rules of Sailing* apply to S and P, and P is required to keep clear under rule 10 (which is in Part 2 of the RRS). S is entitled to redress because S's score in the race is made significantly worse by being physically damaged by P who was breaking a rule of Part 2 [see rule 62.1(b)].

The preamble to Part 2 also states that a boat not racing shall not be penalized for breaking a rule of Part 2, with one exception that does not apply in this scenario. The definition Racing states in part, "A boat is racing from her preparatory signal..." Therefore, because the collision occurs before their preparatory signal, S and P are not "racing" at the time and therefore P cannot be penalized for her breach of rule 10.

Answers are based on *The Racing Rules of Sailing for 2009 – 2012*. *Dave Perry's 100 Best Racing Rules Quizzes* is published by the United States Sailing Association (US SAILING). For a comprehensive explanation of the rules, read Dave Perry's *Understanding the Racing Rules of Sailing through 2012* which also is available from US SAILING — 1 (800) 877-2451 or www.ussailing.org

Quiz 78

Thirty seconds prior to the start, Boat P (on port tack) is passing close by to leeward of Boat S (on starboard tack) and accidentally gets her bow tangled in S's mainsheet. The two boats become locked together for approximately one minute. Though the collision causes no injury or physical damage to S, S finishes very poorly due to her late start. She protests P and requests redress. You are on the protest committee; how would you decide this?

ANSWER

Boat P is penalized for breaking rule 10, On Opposite Tacks. However, Boat S's request for redress is denied. Rule 62.1(b), Redress, applies only to injury to a person or "physical" damage; i.e., damage to a boat's hull, equipment, sails, etc. In this case S sustained no injury or physical damage, and therefore is not entitled to redress. (See ISAF Case 110.)

Answers are based on *The Racing Rules of Sailing for 2009 – 2012. Dave Perry's 100 Best Racing Rules Quizzes* is published by the United States Sailing Association (US SAILING). For a comprehensive explanation of the rules, read Dave Perry's *Understanding the Racing Rules of Sailing through 2012* which also is available from US SAILING — 1 (800) 877-2451 or www.ussailing.org

Quiz 79

Immediately after the start, the race committee chairman sees a collision between Boat P (a port-tack boat) and Boat S (a starboard-tack boat). Neither boat protests or acknowledges fault. Having no doubt that P is in the wrong, the race committee chairman scores P "DSQ" for that race, but that fact does not become known to any of the competitors, including P, until the race committee posts the scores the following morning. P immediately requests redress under rule 62.1(a), Redress, claiming she has no idea why she has been scored "DSQ." You are on the protest committee; how would you decide this?

ANSWER

Boat P is reinstated in the race under rule 64.2, Decisions on Redress. Though the request for redress is delivered after the time limit in rule 62.2, Redress, there is a good reason for the protest committee to extend this time limit, which is that P had no knowledge of the race committee's action until the following morning. Rule 62.2 requires the protest committee to extend the time limit when there is good reason to do so.

Rule 63.1, Requirement for a Hearing, states, "A boat…shall not be penalized without a hearing…" Therefore, because the race committee acts improperly by disqualifying P from the race without a hearing, and because this action makes her score in the race significantly worse through no fault of her own, P is entitled to redress under rule 64.2; and the most fair arrangement is to reinstate P to her finishing place. The correct procedure for the race committee to follow in this case is to protest P, as rule 60.2, Right to Protest; Right to Request Redress or Rule 69 Action, allows.

Answers are based on *The Racing Rules of Sailing for 2009 – 2012. Dave Perry's 100 Best Racing Rules Quizzes* is published by the United States Sailing Association (US SAILING). For a comprehensive explanation of the rules, read Dave Perry's *Understanding the Racing Rules of Sailing through 2012* which also is available from US SAILING — 1 (800) 877-2451 or www.ussailing.org

Quiz 80

In a post-race conversation, the helmsman of Boat X complains to a member of the protest committee that he clearly saw another boat in his race, Boat Y, touch the gybe mark and not take a penalty turn. The protest committee member therefore decides to protest Y for an alleged breach of rule 31, Touching a Mark. Y is informed that she is being protested, and the protest is filed within the time limit. You are on the protest committee; how would you decide this?

ANSWER

The protest is not valid and therefore its hearing should be closed under rule 63.5, Hearings: Validity of the Protest or Request for Redress. Rule 60.3, Right to Protest; Right to Request Redress or Rule 69 Action, governs the action by the protest committee in this case, and states that a protest committee cannot protest as a result of a report by a competitor from another boat (with an exception that doesn't apply in this case). Because all the requirements for a protest have not been met, the protest is not valid. When competitors witness alleged breaches of the rules, and they want the incident to go to a hearing, they must act themselves according to rule 60.1, Right to Protest; Right to Request Redress or Rule 69 Action.

Answers are based on *The Racing Rules of Sailing for 2009 – 2012*. *Dave Perry's 100 Best Racing Rules Quizzes* is published by the United States Sailing Association (US SAILING). For a comprehensive explanation of the rules, read Dave Perry's *Understanding the Racing Rules of Sailing through 2012* which also is available from US SAILING — 1 (800) 877-2451 or www.ussailing.org

Quiz 81

Boat L (a leeward boat) and Boat W (a windward boat) are sailing close-hauled about four feet apart on parallel courses immediately after the start. The wind is very light and the boats have little steerageway. Suddenly, a nearby powerboat guns its engine, and the resulting wake causes L and W to make contact momentarily. L protests W under rule 11, On the Same Tack, Overlapped, and delivers the written protest to the race office. The protest committee finds that the contact was "minor and unavoidable," and disallows L's protest. L appeals. You are on the appeals committee; how would you decide this?

ANSWER

Boat L's appeal is upheld; the protest committee is required to find facts and make their decision (rule 64.1, Decisions: Penalties and Exoneration). Rule 63.1, Requirements for a Hearing, requires the protest committee to hear L's protest. Rule 63.1 allows a protesting boat to request that her protest be withdrawn prior to the hearing, but in this case L did not ask to withdraw her protest. The fact that the contact was "minor and unavoidable" is immaterial; contact is contact. Therefore W is penalized for failing to keep clear of L under rule 11.

Answers are based on *The Racing Rules of Sailing for 2009 – 2012. Dave Perry's 100 Best Racing Rules Quizzes* is published by the United States Sailing Association (US SAILING). For a comprehensive explanation of the rules, read Dave Perry's *Understanding the Racing Rules of Sailing through 2012* which also is available from US SAILING — 1 (800) 877-2451 or www.ussailing.org

Quiz 82

Boat X protests Boat Y. At the hearing, Boat X submits two written reports from witnesses who are unable to attend the hearing. The protest committee reads the reports aloud, over Y's objection, and continues with the hearing. Y is disqualified and appeals. You are on the appeals committee; how would you decide this?

ANSWER

Boat Y's appeal is sustained. The hearing is invalid and Y is reinstated in the race. Rule 63.6, Taking Evidence and Finding Facts, states that a party to a hearing may question any person who gives evidence. Y was denied this right, thereby invalidating the hearing. (See US SAILING Appeal 63.)

Answers are based on *The Racing Rules of Sailing for 2009 – 2012. Dave Perry's 100 Best Racing Rules Quizzes* is published by the United States Sailing Association (US SAILING). For a comprehensive explanation of the rules, read Dave Perry's *Understanding the Racing Rules of Sailing through 2012* which also is available from US SAILING — 1 (800) 877-2451 or www.ussailing.org

Quiz 83

Boats L and W round a mark very close together but with no contact, and L touches the mark. L immediately hails "Protest," displays her protest flag and does a penalty turn. W continues sailing the course without protesting. At the protest hearing, the protest committee refuses to hear L's protest, claiming that because she took a penalty she must have been at fault thereby making the protest a moot point. L appeals. You are on the appeals committee; how would you decide this?

ANSWER

Boat L's appeal is upheld; the protest committee must hear L's protest. Rule 63.1, Requirement for a Hearing, requires the protest committee to hear the protest. Furthermore, the fact that L took a penalty does not preclude her from protesting W, nor is it an admission of guilt. In the hearing, if the protest committee finds that W is at fault, she is to be penalized. (The fact that L took a penalty cannot be undone; see US SAILING Appeal 86). However, if the protest committee finds that W did not foul L, L has already exonerated herself for breaking rule 31, Touching a Mark.

Answers are based on *The Racing Rules of Sailing for 2009 – 2012*. *Dave Perry's 100 Best Racing Rules Quizzes* is published by the United States Sailing Association (US SAILING). For a comprehensive explanation of the rules, read Dave Perry's *Understanding the Racing Rules of Sailing through 2012* which also is available from US SAILING — 1 (800) 877-2451 or www.ussailing.org

Quiz 84

During the hearing of a valid protest concerning a crowded mark rounding, Boat X gives testimony as a witness. After a short round of questions from the parties and the protest committee, X is thanked for her time and excused. During the deliberation, the protest committee decides that X is the outside boat and, based on her testimony, is the boat that caused the problem by failing to provide enough mark-room as required by rule 18.2(b), Giving Mark-Room. Acting under rule 64.1(a), Penalties and Exoneration, the protest committee disqualifies X. X appeals. You are on the appeals committee; how would you decide this?

ANSWER

The decision of the protest committee is changed, and Boat X is reinstated in the race. X is entitled by rule 63.1, Requirement For a Hearing, to a hearing before being penalized under rule 64.1(a). The protest committee failed to give her this. Rule 61.1(c), Protest Requirements: Informing the Protestee, permits the protest committee in this case to protest X. However, the protest committee is required to inform X as soon as reasonably possible of its intention to protest, put its protest in writing, and inform her of the time and place of the hearing (rules 61.1(c), 61.2, Protest Contents and 63, Hearings).

Answers are based on *The Racing Rules of Sailing for 2009 – 2012*. *Dave Perry's 100 Best Racing Rules Quizzes* is published by the United States Sailing Association (US SAILING). For a comprehensive explanation of the rules, read Dave Perry's *Understanding the Racing Rules of Sailing through 2012* which also is available from US SAILING — 1 (800) 877-2451 or www.ussailing.org

Quiz 85

At the start of the race, the race committee makes the starting signal three seconds late and notes that at that time four of the 20 boats are on the course side of the starting line. After the race, upon seeing that they are scored OCS, the four boats request redress under rule 62.1(a), Redress, claiming that their race scores have been made significantly worse by the improper action of the race committee. The protest committee finds this to be the case and, acting under rule 64.2, Decisions on Redress, orders the race abandoned and resailed. Boat Y, not one of the four boats involved in the redress hearing, vehemently disagrees and appeals, claiming that the protest committee's decision is wrong, that it had been a perfectly fair race, and that the correct decision is to simply reinstate the four boats to their actual finishing places. You are on the association appeals committee; how would you decide this?

ANSWER

The appeal is not heard because Boat Y has no right to appeal. Rule 70.1, Appeals and Requests to a National Authority, states that a boat must be a "party to a hearing" to appeal. Under the definition Party, a boat is a "party to a hearing" when she is a protesting boat, a protested boat, any other boat that might be penalized (i.e., given a penalty), or a boat that has requested redress (see US SAILING Appeal 64). Y is none of these. When a boat feels that her score in a race has been made significantly worse by an improper action of the protest committee, she can request redress herself under 62.1(a) provided she does so within the time limit in rule 62.2. She can then appeal that decision if she desires. (See ISAF Cases 55 and 71.)

Answers are based on *The Racing Rules of Sailing for 2009 – 2012*. Dave Perry's *100 Best Racing Rules Quizzes* is published by the United States Sailing Association (US SAILING). For a comprehensive explanation of the rules, read Dave Perry's *Understanding the Racing Rules of Sailing through 2012* which also is available from US SAILING — 1 (800) 877-2451 or www.ussailing.org

Quiz 86

A yacht club's yearly club championship finals comes down to the last race in which there is a controversial protest between Boats X and Y. The notice of race and the sailing instructions for the event state explicitly that there will be no appeal from any decisions of the protest committee. The protest committee is composed of the yacht club's finest rules experts though none are certified judges. X loses the protest and appeals. You are on the appeals committee; will you accept her appeal?

ANSWER

Boat X's appeal is accepted and will be decided on its merits. Rule 70.1, Appeals and Requests to a National Authority, states that decisions of a protest committee may be appealed provided that the right of appeal has not been denied based on the exceptions in rule 70.5 (none of which apply in this case). The significant exceptions are: 1) when the decision is from a properly constituted international jury; 2) when it is essential to determine promptly the result of a race that will qualify a boat to compete in a later stage of the event or a subsequent event; and 3) when a national authority so prescribes for a particular event open only to entrants under its own jurisdiction.

Answers are based on *The Racing Rules of Sailing for 2009 – 2012*. *Dave Perry's 100 Best Racing Rules Quizzes* is published by the United States Sailing Association (US SAILING). For a comprehensive explanation of the rules, read Dave Perry's *Understanding the Racing Rules of Sailing through 2012* which also is available from US SAILING — 1 (800) 877-2451 or www.ussailing.org

Quiz 87

The class rules for a 25-foot boat state that racing rule 61.1(a), Protest Requirements: Informing the Protestee, is changed such that boats do not have to display a protest flag in class events. The notice of race and the sailing instructions for the class national championship both state that the class rules will be in effect, but list no specific racing rule changes. Boat Y protests Boat X for a windward mark incident. Y hails "Protest" but doesn't display a flag. The protest committee hears the protest over X's objection that the protest isn't valid and disqualifies X, who then appeals. You are on the appeals committee; how would you decide this?

ANSWER

Boat X's appeal is upheld and she is reinstated in the race. Y did not display a protest flag as required by rule 61.1(a); therefore her protest is not valid, and the protest hearing should have been closed (see rule 63.5, Hearings: Validity of the Protest or Request for Redress). Class rules can only change racing rules 42 and 49-54 [see rule 86.1(c)]. As rule 61.1 is not a rule that class rules are allowed to change, the only way rule 61.1 can be changed is by a specific reference to it in the sailing instructions [see rule 86.1(b)].

Answers are based on *The Racing Rules of Sailing for 2009 – 2012. Dave Perry's 100 Best Racing Rules Quizzes* is published by the United States Sailing Association (US SAILING). For a comprehensive explanation of the rules, read Dave Perry's *Understanding the Racing Rules of Sailing through 2012* which also is available from US SAILING — 1 (800) 877-2451 or www.ussailing.org

Quiz 88

The sailing instructions simply state: "Six races are scheduled of which three shall be completed to constitute a series." At the end of the regatta the scores are posted. Boat A, believing she has finished third overall, finds herself listed in sixth place. She notices that the scores have been calculated without dropping each boat's worst score. She points this out to the scorer who replies that the sailing instructions do not provide for a "throw-out race." A requests redress. You are on the protest committee; how would you decide this?

ANSWER

The race committee is to score the regatta discarding each boat's worst score in accordance with rule A2, Series Score. See rule 90.3(a), Scoring. Rule A2 states, "Each boat's series score will be the total of her race scores excluding her worst score…" If the race committee intended for boats to count each score, it would have had to specifically say so in the sailing instructions.

Answers are based on *The Racing Rules of Sailing for 2009 – 2012. Dave Perry's 100 Best Racing Rules Quizzes* is published by the United States Sailing Association (US SAILING). For a comprehensive explanation of the rules, read Dave Perry's *Understanding the Racing Rules of Sailing through 2012* which also is available from US SAILING — 1 (800) 877-2451 or www.ussailing.org

Quizzes 89-100

Advanced Rules Quizzes

Team Racing, Match Racing,
Scoring and other rules
situations

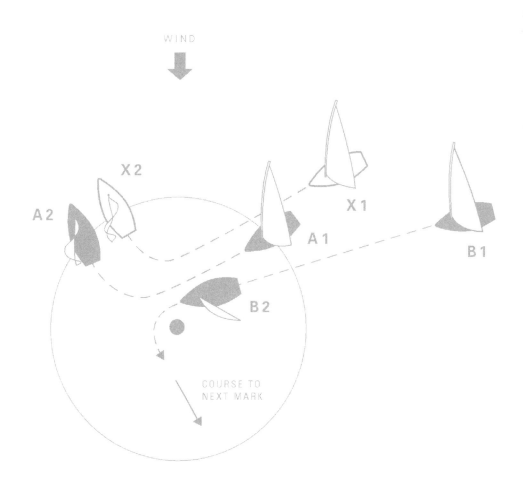

Quiz 89

In a team race, Boats A and X, on opposite teams, are on starboard tack within one length of each other but not overlapped as they approach a downwind mark to be left to port. When four lengths from the mark, and with X steering a course to leeward of her, A sails below her proper course to prevent X from being able to establish a leeward overlap and become entitled to mark-room. X protests. You are on the protest committee; how would you decide this?

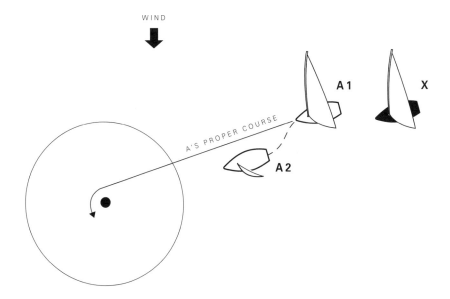

ANSWER

Boat X's protest is disallowed. There is no rule requiring A to not sail below her proper course in this situation. A is clear ahead of X and therefore is the right-of-way boat under rule 12, On the Same Tack, Not Overlapped. When she changes course she needs to give X room to keep clear under rule 16.1, Changing Course, which she does.

Answers are based on *The Racing Rules of Sailing for 2009 – 2012. Dave Perry's 100 Best Racing Rules Quizzes* is published by the United States Sailing Association (US SAILING). For a comprehensive explanation of the rules, read Dave Perry's *Understanding the Racing Rules of Sailing through 2012* which also is available from US SAILING — 1 (800) 877-2451 or www.ussailing.org

Quiz 90

In a team race, Boats A, X and B are on starboard tack approaching a downwind mark to be left to port. The course to the next mark is a beam reach on port tack, meaning that the proper course for all three boats is to gybe around the mark. Boats A and B are on the same team. When A reaches the zone, none of the boats are overlapped; and when X reaches the zone, B is still clear astern of her. A slows dramatically and X overlaps her to windward. A then sails past the point where her proper course is to gybe around the mark and then luffs and begins sailing away from the mark. X is able to keep clear by also luffing and sailing away from the mark. B passes astern of both boats and rounds the mark. X protests A for not sailing her proper course around the mark; and protests B for taking room when she was not entitled to it. You are on the protest committee; how would you decide this?

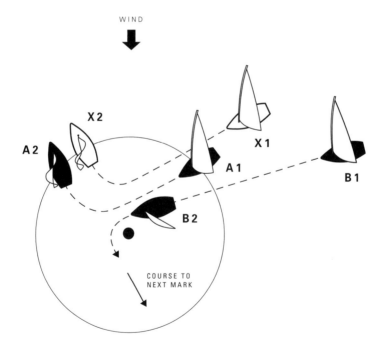

WIND

X 2

A 2

X 1

A 1

B 1

B 2

COURSE TO
NEXT MARK

Answers are based on *The Racing Rules of Sailing for 2009 – 2012*. *Dave Perry's 100 Best Racing Rules Quizzes* is published by the United States Sailing Association (US SAILING). For a comprehensive explanation of the rules, read Dave Perry's *Understanding the Racing Rules of Sailing through 2012* which also is available from US SAILING — 1 (800) 877-2451 or www.ussailing.org

ANSWER

Both of Boat X's protests are disallowed. Team racing is sailed under *The Racing Rules of Sailing* as changed by Appendix D — Team Racing Rules. Rule D1.1(c) says that rule 18.4, Mark-Room: Gybing, is deleted. Therefore A is not required to gybe to continue sailing her proper course around the mark. As leeward boat, A has the right of way under rule 11, On the Same Tack, Overlapped. And when she changes course, she gives X room to keep clear as required by rule 16.1, Changing Course.

Regarding B's actions, because she is clear astern of X when X reaches the zone, she is required to give X mark-room under rule 18.2(b), Mark-Room: Giving Mark-Room. And though she subsequently becomes overlapped inside X, she is not entitled to mark-room [see rule 18.2(c)]. However B breaks no rule by passing between the mark and X provided that X does not have to take any action to avoid her, which in this case she doesn't. (See ISAF Case 63.)

Answers are based on *The Racing Rules of Sailing for 2009 – 2012. Dave Perry's 100 Best Racing Rules Quizzes* is published by the United States Sailing Association (US SAILING). For a comprehensive explanation of the rules, read Dave Perry's *Understanding the Racing Rules of Sailing through 2012* which also is available from US SAILING — 1 (800) 877-2451 or www.ussailing.org

Quiz 91

In a team race, Boats A and X, on opposite teams, are approaching a wind-wind mark to be left to starboard. A is on starboard tack and several lengths ahead of X. As A reaches the zone, X is passing astern of her by two lengths. A stops her boat to prepare to trap X at the mark. X tacks onto starboard, catches up to A, overlaps her to windward and calls for room at the mark. A bears away to avoid X and protests. In the protest hearing X claims that A was already within two lengths of the mark when X completed her tack onto starboard tack, and therefore rule 18.2(b), Mark-Room: Giving Mark-Room, does not apply. You are on the protest committee; how would you decide this?

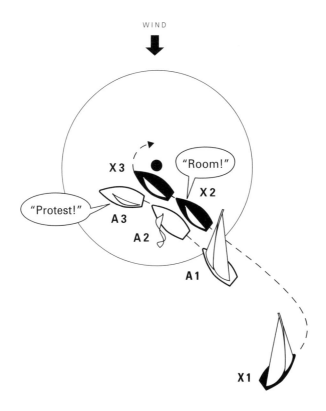

ANSWER

Boat X is disqualified. Team racing is sailed under *The Racing Rules of Sailing* as changed by Appendix D — Team Racing Rules. Rule D1.1(b) changes the first sentence of rule 18.2(b) as follows: "If a boat is clear ahead when she reaches the zone, or she later becomes clear ahead when another boat passes head to wind, the boat clear astern at that moment shall thereafter give her mark-room." While A and X are on opposite tacks, the terms "clear ahead" and "clear astern" do not apply (see definition Clear Astern and Clear Ahead; Overlap). The terms begin to apply when X passes head to wind and is on starboard tack. At that moment, A becomes clear ahead; and although she is already within two lengths of the mark, rule 18.2(b) as changed by rule D1.1(b) requires X to give her mark-room, which X fails to do. X also fails to keep clear as the windward boat under rule 11, On the Same Tack, Overlapped.

Answers are based on *The Racing Rules of Sailing for 2009 – 2012. Dave Perry's 100 Best Racing Rules Quizzes* is published by the United States Sailing Association (US SAILING). For a comprehensive explanation of the rules, read Dave Perry's *Understanding the Racing Rules of Sailing through 2012* which also is available from US SAILING — 1 (800) 877-2451 or www.ussailing.org

Quiz 92

In a match race, Boat S on starboard tack and Boat P on port tack are approaching a windward mark to be left to starboard. S enters the zone, crosses P by one length and tacks. After the tack, S is half a length ahead of P. P holds her course and becomes overlapped to leeward of P and calls for mark-room. S luffs to avoid a collision and protests. P rounds the mark without hitting it. You are the umpire; what call would you make?

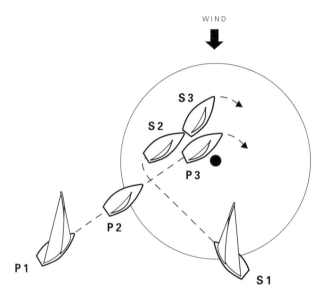

ANSWER

Boat P is penalized. Match racing is sailed under *The Racing Rules of Sailing* as changed by Appendix C — Match Racing Rules. Rule C2.6 changes rule 18.3. It says that if one boat changes tack inside the zone and the other boat can by luffing avoid becoming overlapped inside her, then when the boat that tacked completes her tack, she is entitled to mark-room. After S completes her tack, P can luff and avoid becoming overlapped inside of S. Therefore under rule C2.6(b) S is entitled to mark-room from P, which P failed to give.

Answers are based on *The Racing Rules of Sailing for 2009 – 2012*. *Dave Perry's 100 Best Racing Rules Quizzes* is published by the United States Sailing Association (US SAILING). For a comprehensive explanation of the rules, read Dave Perry's *Understanding the Racing Rules of Sailing through 2012* which also is available from US SAILING — 1 (800) 877-2451 or www.ussailing.org

Quiz 93

Boats PL and PW do not have very good starts, and tack onto port tack to find clear air. They are approaching the race committee boat at the starboard end of the starting line and neither can clear the boat and its anchor line without tacking. PL hails for room to tack at the obstruction, but PW does not reply. PL then tacks, and while she is past head to wind but before she is on a close-hauled course, PW tacks to try to avoid hitting her but the boats collide with no damage or injury. Neither boat protests. Back on shore, before the protest filing time has expired, a member of the race committee informs PL and PW that the race committee is protesting both PL and PW. You are on the protest committee; how would you decide this?

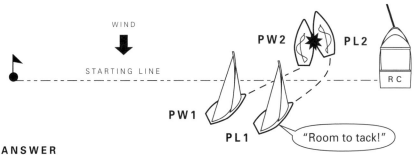

ANSWER

Boat PL is penalized for breaking rule 13, While Tacking, and rule 14, Avoiding Contact. The race committee may protest a boat under rule 60.2, Right to Protest; Right to Request Redress or Rule 69 Action. The race committee boat and its anchor line are an obstruction to PL and PW. However the preamble to Section C, At Marks and Obstructions, states that Section C rules do not apply at a starting mark surrounded by navigable water or at its anchor line when boats are approaching them to start until they have passed them. Rule 20, Room to Tack at an Obstruction, is in Section C. Therefore PL does not have the right to hail PW for room to tack, nor does PW have to respond to such a hail. When PL passed head to wind, she was required to keep clear of PW under rule 13 which she failed to do. PL also broke rule 14 by tacking so close to PW that there was contact. PW tried to avoid PL by tacking but was unable to. Therefore PW does not break rule 14.

Answers are based on *The Racing Rules of Sailing for 2009 – 2012. Dave Perry's 100 Best Racing Rules Quizzes* is published by the United States Sailing Association (US SAILING). For a comprehensive explanation of the rules, read Dave Perry's *Understanding the Racing Rules of Sailing through 2012* which also is available from US SAILING — 1 (800) 877-2451 or www.ussailing.org

Quiz 94

Two 35-foot boats, PA and PB, are approaching the starting line on a port-tack reach for a downwind start. The wind is a steady 15 knots from the north and there is no current. The course to the first mark is 225 degrees. There are no other boats in the near vicinity of PA and PB. At 20 seconds before the starting signal, PB is clear astern of PA and aiming at the race committee boat. At the starting signal, PB is overlapped and about half-a-length to leeward of PA, and is holding her course towards the committee boat. Five seconds later, PA calls for room at the starting mark and bears away and her boom hits one of PB's crew members in the head causing him to bleed profusely. At the time, PA is about one length from the committee boat. Neither boat says "Protest" or flies a protest flag. PA immediately gets clear of PB, takes a Two-Turns Penalty and continues in the race. PB immediately gybes and attends to the bleeding crew while continuing in the race. Soon after the race, PB informs PA that she is protesting her. You are on the protest committee; how would you decide this?

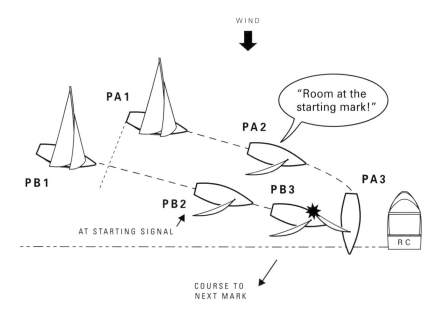

Answers are based on *The Racing Rules of Sailing for 2009 – 2012*. *Dave Perry's 100 Best Racing Rules Quizzes* is published by the United States Sailing Association (US SAILING). For a comprehensive explanation of the rules, read Dave Perry's *Understanding the Racing Rules of Sailing through 2012* which also is available from US SAILING — 1 (800) 877-2451 or www.ussailing.org

ANSWER

Both boats PA and PB are penalized. Because it is obvious to both boats that the incident results in injury, neither boat is required to hail "Protest" or fly a protest flag in order to protest. PB informs PA of her intent to protest within the time limit for filing protests (see rule 61.1(a)(3), Informing the Protestee).

Though the boats were near the race committee boat, the preamble to Section C, At Marks and Obstructions, states that Section C rules do not apply at a starting mark surrounded by navigable water or at its anchor line when boats are approaching them to start until they have passed them. Therefore rule 18, Mark-Room, did not apply. While the two boats are overlapped, PA is required to keep clear of PB under rule 11, On the Same Tack, Overlapped. By bearing away and having contact with PB, she fails to do so. The fact that PB is improperly sailing above her proper course (see below) does not change the fact that PA is required to keep clear of her. In addition to breaking rule 11, PA also breaks rule 14, Avoiding Contact. Furthermore, rule 44.1(b), Penalties at the Time of an Incident: Taking a Penalty, says that a boat that breaks a rule and causes injury as a result must retire from the race; she cannot exonerate herself by taking a Two-Turns Penalty. A person who is bleeding profusely from the head is injured. Because PA did not retire, she also breaks rule 44.1(b).

PB becomes overlapped to leeward of PA from clear astern. Though holding right of way under rule 11, PB is required to sail no higher than her proper course under rule 17, On the Same Tack; Proper Course. A boat does not have a proper course before the starting signal (see definition Proper Course). But after the starting signal, PB is required to sail no higher than her proper course. In the absence of PA (the other boat referred to in rule 17) and absent any other mitigating factors of which there are none, PB's fastest course to the first mark is to gybe and head towards the mark. Five seconds go by after the starting signal with no attempt by PB to bear away and gybe. Therefore she breaks rule 17 by sailing above her proper course.

Answers are based on *The Racing Rules of Sailing for 2009–2012*. *Dave Perry's 100 Best Racing Rules Quizzes* is published by the United States Sailing Association (US SAILING). For a comprehensive explanation of the rules, read Dave Perry's *Understanding the Racing Rules of Sailing through 2012* which also is available from US SAILING — 1 (800) 877-2451 or www.ussailing.org

Quiz 95

Four boats are approaching a port-hand windward mark, two on starboard tack (SA and SB) and two on port tack (PW and PL). One of the starboard-tack boats (SB) is approximately two lengths behind the other starboard-tack boat (SA) and one length to windward of her. The two port-tack boats (PW and PL) are both ducking SA, with PL to leeward and about three-quarters of a length ahead of PW. As the boats are passing astern of SA, PL hails PW for room to tack to clear SB. Because PW can't tack right then without hitting SA, PW does not reply. PL immediately luffs sharply to try to avoid SB, but SB needs to luff to avoid hitting PL. PW tries to avoid PL but can't and there is slight contact between them with no damage or injury. SB protests PL for breaking rule 10 (port/starboard), and PL protests PW for failing to respond to her hail under rule 20.1 (hailing for room to tack at an obstruction). You are on the protest committee; how would you decide this?

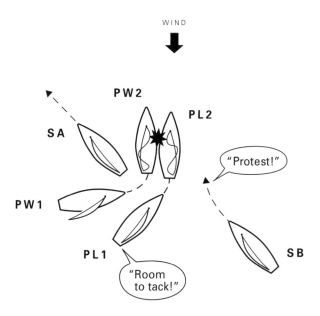

ANSWER

Boat PL is penalized for breaking rule 10, On Opposite Tacks, rule 16.1, Changing Course, and rule 20.1, Room to Tack at an Obstruction. PW breaks rule 11, On the Same Tack, Overlapped, but is exonerated under rule 64.1(c), Decisions: Penalties and Exoneration, because she is compelled to break rule 11 by PL's rule breaches.

Both SA and SB are obstructions to PW and PL because both PW and PL are required to keep clear of them under rule 10 (see definition Obstruction). When PW and PL are passing astern of SA, they are overlapped. Rule 19.2(b), Giving Room at an Obstruction, requires PL to give PW room to pass SA, which she is doing.

Safety requires PL to make a substantial course change to avoid SB; and rule 20.1 gives her the right to hail PW for room to tack to avoid SB. However, rule 20.1(a) requires PL to give PW time to respond to the hail before tacking. One of PW's options for responding is to tack as soon as possible [rule 20.1(b)]. When PL hails, it is not possible for PW to tack due to her proximity to SA. As soon as she can she begins tacking, but PL has already started to tack and the boats collide. Therefore PL fails to give PW time to respond before tacking. Furthermore, when PL luffs, i.e., changes course, she fails to give PW room to keep clear, thereby breaking rule 16.1.

Regarding the contact, it is not possible for PW to avoid contact, so she does not break rule 14, Avoiding Contact. PL on the other hand can avoid contact with PW by passing astern of SB instead of tacking. Therefore PL breaks rule 14, but is not penalized under that rule because she is the right-of-way boat and the contact does not cause damage or injury [see rule 14(b)].

Answers are based on *The Racing Rules of Sailing for 2009 – 2012. Dave Perry's 100 Best Racing Rules Quizzes* is published by the United States Sailing Association (US SAILING). For a comprehensive explanation of the rules, read Dave Perry's *Understanding the Racing Rules of Sailing through 2012* which also is available from US SAILING — 1 (800) 877-2451 or www.ussailing.org

Quiz 96

Boats SW and SL are sailing downwind on starboard tack with SW overlapped to windward of SL. Just ahead is Boat X which has just been righted after capsizing. X is on port tack and the sailors are climbing back on board. SL bears away to pass by the bow of X as does SW. There is not enough space for SW to pass between SL and X, and SW's boom hits SL's starboard shroud (no damage or injury). Both boats protest. You are on the protest committee; how would you decide this?

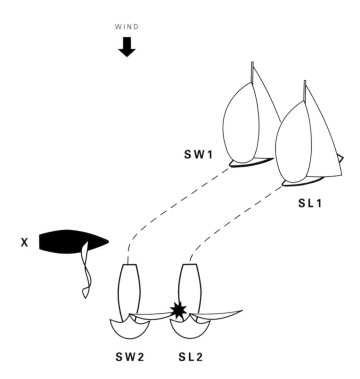

ANSWER

Boat SL is penalized for breaking rule 19.2(b), Giving Room at an Obstruction. Because X has not regained control after capsizing, both SL and SW are required to avoid her (see rule 22, Capsized, Anchored or Aground; Rescuing). Therefore X ranks as an obstruction to both of them (see definition Obstruction). Because SW is overlapped with SL and SL is passing astern of X, SW is entitled to room from SL to pass the obstruction on the same side [see rule 19.2(b)]. SL fails to provide that room and breaks 19.2(b).

Regarding rule 14, Avoiding Contact, clearly SL breaks it by not bearing away far enough to provide room for SW to pass between her and X without hitting either. SW need not act to avoid contact until it is clear that SL is failing to provide room. At that point it is likely that it is not reasonably possible for SW to avoid hitting SL, so SW does not break rule 14. However, in either case neither boat can be penalized under rule 14 because there is no damage or injury. SL is a right-of-way boat and SW is a boat entitled to room [see rule 14(b)]. Note: the fact that SL is required to give room to SW under rule 19.2(b) does not change the fact that SL is the right-of-way boat under rule 11, On the Same Tack, Overlapped (see the preamble to Part 2, Section A – Right of Way).

Answers are based on *The Racing Rules of Sailing for 2009 – 2012. Dave Perry's 100 Best Racing Rules Quizzes* is published by the United States Sailing Association (US SAILING). For a comprehensive explanation of the rules, read Dave Perry's *Understanding the Racing Rules of Sailing through 2012* which also is available from US SAILING — 1 (800) 877-2451 or www.ussailing.org

Quiz 97

Boat P (on port tack) is running downwind and on a parallel course with a dock less than one length away. Boat S (on starboard tack) is fast approaching P from clear astern and hails, "Starboard!" Approximately five seconds later, S makes minor contact with P's transom (no damage or injury) and protests. You are on the protest committee; how would you decide this?

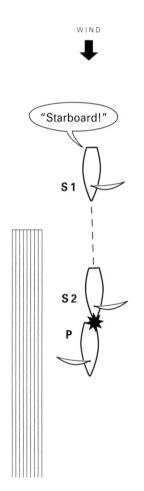

ANSWER

Boat P is penalized for breaking rules 10, On Opposite Tacks, and rule 14, Avoiding Contact. Though the boats are passing an obstruction (the dock), they are not overlapped, so no part of rule 19.2, Room to Pass an Obstruction: Giving Room at an Obstruction, applies. Therefore, although P is clear ahead when she first reaches the obstruction, she gets no protection from rule 19.2 once she and S begin passing the obstruction, and she must therefore keep clear of S under rule 10.

Regarding rule 14, it is reasonably possible for P to avoid contact with S by moving out of her way; she fails to do so and breaks rule 14 as a result. It is similarly reasonably possible for S to avoid contact with P, so she also breaks rule 14. However, a right-of-way boat can be penalized for breaking rule 14 only when the contact causes damage or injury. In this case it caused neither; therefore S is not penalized.

Answers are based on *The Racing Rules of Sailing for 2009 – 2012*. *Dave Perry's 100 Best Racing Rules Quizzes* is published by the United States Sailing Association (US SAILING). For a comprehensive explanation of the rules, read Dave Perry's *Understanding the Racing Rules of Sailing through 2012* which also is available from US SAILING — 1 (800) 877-2451 or www.ussailing.org

Quiz 98

Approximately 30 seconds before the leeward mark, Boat X releases the spinnaker guy from the spinnaker pole, and a crew member holds the guy by hand, leaning out over the lifelines so as to maximize the distance between the hull and the guy until the spinnaker is lowered. Lifelines are required by class rules. Boat Y protests X for this. You are on the protest committee; how would you decide this?

ANSWER

Boat Y's protest is disallowed. Rule 49.2, Crew Position, permits the torso of a crew member to be outside the lifelines briefly when performing a necessary task. It is necessary to continue controlling the spinnaker once the spinnaker pole is down, and the crew was over the lifelines for only a brief amount of time. (See US SAILING Appeal 72.)

Answers are based on *The Racing Rules of Sailing for 2009 – 2012. Dave Perry's 100 Best Racing Rules Quizzes* is published by the United States Sailing Association (US SAILING). For a comprehensive explanation of the rules, read Dave Perry's *Understanding the Racing Rules of Sailing through 2012* which also is available from US SAILING — 1 (800) 877-2451 or www.ussailing.org

Quiz 99

During the hearing of a request for redress, the protest committee learns that Boat X has touched a mark during the race. The protest committee protests X, giving her time to prepare, etc., holds a protest hearing with X in attendance, and disqualifies her for breaking rule 31, Touching a Mark. X appeals. You are on the appeals committee; how would you decide this?

ANSWER

Boat X's appeal is sustained and the protest committee's decision is reversed. Boat X is reinstated in the race. Rule 60.3, Right to Protest; Right to Request Redress or Rule 69 Action, says that the protest committee cannot protest a boat as a result of information in a request for redress.

Answers are based on *The Racing Rules of Sailing for 2009 – 2012. Dave Perry's 100 Best Racing Rules Quizzes* is published by the United States Sailing Association (US SAILING). For a comprehensive explanation of the rules, read Dave Perry's *Understanding the Racing Rules of Sailing through 2012* which also is available from US SAILING — 1 (800) 877-2451 or www.ussailing.org

Quiz 100

The sailing instructions for a race simply state: "Six races are scheduled of which three shall be completed to constitute a series." Boat P's scores are (in race order): 3-2-3-4-1-6. Boat Q's scores are (also in race order): 4-8-2-1-3-3. You are the scorer; which boat beats the other?

ANSWER

Boat Q beats Boat P. Rule 90.3(a), Scoring, says that the race committee shall score a series as provided in Appendix A – Scoring, using the Low Point System unless the sailing instructions specify some other system. Rule A2, Series Scores, says that each boat's score shall be the total of her race scores excluding her worst race unless the sailing instructions specify some other arrangement. Rule A8, Series Ties, says that first you see who has the greater number of firsts, then seconds, etc. excluding the worst race. Boats P and Q each have a 1-2-3-3-4. Then you see who beats whom in the last race, using all the race scores including the excluded one. Q beats P in race 6 and is therefore the winner.

Answers are based on *The Racing Rules of Sailing for 2009 – 2012*. *Dave Perry's 100 Best Racing Rules Quizzes* is published by the United States Sailing Association (US SAILING). For a comprehensive explanation of the rules, read Dave Perry's *Understanding the Racing Rules of Sailing through 2012* which also is available from US SAILING — 1 (800) 877-2451 or www.ussailing.org

How to Prepare a Protest and a Defense

Bill Ficker on how to be successful in the protest room, plus US SAILING's Protest Form

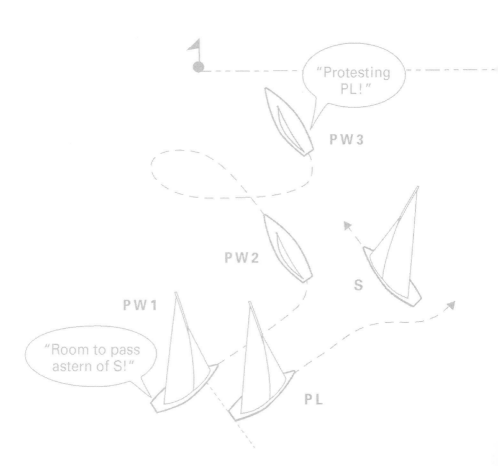

How to Prepare a Protest and a Defense

BY BILL FICKER

Edited by Mary Savage

NOTE BY DAVE PERRY

In the 1981 Congressional cup, I was Russell Long's tactician and we were disqualified in a protest for tacking too close. After the series was completed, Bill Ficker, who was on the jury, came over and volunteered some advice on how we could have presented a bitter defense. Sure enough, two weeks later I was involved in almost exactly the same situation, but this time successfully defended myself applying the principles Bill had described. To anyone who has ever lost a series by being disqualified in a protest hearing, it's clear that developing excellent protest handling skills is as important to winning regattas as having superior boat speed or brilliant tactics. But it's fair to say that among even the best sailors, the protest handling skills are not as refined as they could be, and this is one area we could all improve in.

Bill Ficker is a welcome authority on the subject, based not only on his successful experiences as both a competitor and a judge, but even more importantly because his success is the result of his very organized and thorough approach to what he does, making his presentation full of useful details and easy to follow. As a competitor, Bill has been racing all his life. Growing up in Southern California, he has raced Sabots, Snipes, National One-Designs, Pacific 14 dinghies, and finished second in the Intercollegiate National Championship. Since then

Based on *The Racing Rules of Sailing for 2009 – 2012*. Dave Perry's *100 Best Racing Rules Quizzes* is published by the United States Sailing Association (US SAILING). For a comprehensive explanation of the rules, read Dave Perry's *Understanding the Racing Rules of Sailing through 2012* which also is available from US SAILING — 1 (800) 877-2451 or www.ussailing.org

he has won the Star Worlds, Class A of the SORC skippering "Charisma," and the Congressional Cup. In 1970 he successfully defended the America's Cup as skipper of "Intrepid." As a judge, he has served on the jury for the Congressional Cup, California Cup, San Diego Lipton Cup, and numerous other series over the years. He was a US SAILING-certified Senior Judge for many years and has been a member of the US SAILING Appeals Committee.

Calmness under pressure is certainly one of the keys to success in a protest hearing, as well as confidence in the rules and an analytical attention to all the details of the incident. Through his experiences, Bill has demonstrated a mastery over these elements, and the insights he shares in this piece, if practiced, should prove extremely helpful.

Mary Savage has devoted much of her life to raising the level of judging and rules awareness in the sport. She is an International and US SAILING Judge and member of the US SAILING Racing Rules Committee.

BEFORE TALKING ABOUT THE PROTEST PROCESS, let me say a few words about the actions leading up to the need for a protest. It always seems incredible to me that so many world-class sailors give so much attention to boat speed, crew training, and development of the state-of-the-art equipment and almost totally ignore an equally significant part of their campaign: learning the rules. The rules are the foil in the art of fencing with sailboats and without the sharpest foil and the understanding of how to use it, you are jeopardizing your entire effort or at least compromising it. Insecurity with the rules leads to hesitation on the race course and not only loss of races, but ultimately the respect of your competitors. As everyone who has sailed in top competition knows, the building of a reputation is important in order to dominate a fleet, and those who want to reach the top have to know the rules cold and act with confidence when engaged in a rules conflict. So study the rules and use the US SAILING Appeals Book and ISAF Case Book. By carefully studying the appeals, you will not only gain a better understanding of the rules, but you will also be helped tremendously in the preparation of your protest, especially with regard to the diagrams.

Based on *The Racing Rules of Sailing for 2009 – 2012. Dave Perry's 100 Best Racing Rules Quizzes* is published by the United States Sailing Association (US SAILING). For a comprehensive explanation of the rules, read Dave Perry's *Understanding the Racing Rules of Sailing through 2012* which also is available from US SAILING — 1 (800) 877-2451 or www.ussailing.org

As for protesting, I often hear sailors say that protesting is for others and that they have never been in the protest room in their life. That makes good barroom talk, but the hard facts are that each year sailing, like other sports, is becoming more competitive with more good sailors in each fleet. No longer are fleets dominated by one or two good sailors who can easily stay clear of the others. More close situations are occurring on the starting lines, at turning marks, and throughout the race, so you had better be prepared to finish more races and series in the protest room. Finally, if protests are the result of your being involved in or witnessing a foul, or the result of an honest difference of opinion or differences in observation of a particular situation on the water, they should not have the taint of bad sportsmanship. Competitor enforcement of the rules is the tradition in our sport, and when the rules are not followed, we owe it to ourselves and our fellow competitors, for the quality of the racing, to protest. Remember, for your protest to be valid, it must comply with the requirements in rule 60.1 and rule 61.

Preparation for the Hearing

As any lawyer will tell you, the most important step in winning a case is the preparation. If you are thoroughly prepared, everything else will fall into place.

BOAT PERFORMANCE TABLE

One tool that will dramatically improve both your protest presentation and your tactical decisions on the race course is a table with all your boat performance precisely worked out in feet and seconds. It should include how many feet-per-second your boat travels in varying wind velocities, the approximate speed of your boat on all points of sail, how long it takes your boat to go from one tack or gybe to another in varying wind and sea conditions, how far upwind your boat travels in a tack, how long it takes to accelerate to full speed from a standstill, and how long it takes to make a complete circle in both directions and how large the circle is. Write the table inside the front cover of your rulebook. We'll discuss the reasons for this later.

Based on *The Racing Rules of Sailing for 2009 – 2012. Dave Perry's 100 Best Racing Rules Quizzes* is published by the United States Sailing Association (US SAILING). For a comprehensive explanation of the rules, read Dave Perry's *Understanding the Racing Rules of Sailing through 2012* which also is available from US SAILING — 1 (800) 877-2451 or www.ussailing.org

FILLING OUT THE PROTEST FORM

The protest form you file will usually be the first encounter the jury has with your incident. Therefore, make sure the first impression you make reflects your thoughtfulness, your knowledge of the rules and the boats you are racing, and your care for detail and doing things the right way. Most regattas use the standard US SAILING Protest Form (printed in the back of the rulebook and this book). Take care in filling out each line on the first page. Print clearly, think first to avoid unnecessary cross-outs, and be sure all the information is correct, particularly the names and sail numbers of the other parties to the protest. Also be sure to use a dark pen, and don't get the protest form wet with soggy cuffs or wet hands. Rule 61.2 lists the information required on the protest form. Note, however, that as long as the form identifies the incident, other required details may be corrected before or during the hearing. Rule 61.2(c) asks for the rule(s) alleged to have been broken, but there is no requirement that you must state the correct rule. Rule 64.1(a) reads, "When the protest committee decides that a boat that is a *party* to a protest hearing has broken a *rule*, it shall disqualify her unless some other penalty applies. A penalty shall be imposed whether or not the applicable *rule* was mentioned in the *protest.*"

The diagrams are perhaps a little more difficult if you are not an engineer, architect, or otherwise graphically gifted, but with practice almost anyone can do a good diagram. *Always be sure to work everything out in a rough diagram before putting it on the protest form.* A pad of 8 ½ by 11 quarter-inch graph paper is useful for perfecting your diagram before committing it to the form. (It's also useful for studying the rules and doing sample situation analyses.) Usually the three or four boat positions directly preceding the incident are all that is needed to give the jury a clear picture of how the situation developed. In addition be sure you include all relevant information, such as the strength and direction of the wind and current, the direction to the next (or from the previous) mark, any topography or other obstructions that had an effect, the compass course and speed your boat was going throughout the incident, and the like. Again, exact awareness of time and distance traveled and their relationship to each other are extremely important. The more information you have and the more exact your diagram, the more credibility your case will have in the

Based on *The Racing Rules of Sailing for 2009–2012. Dave Perry's 100 Best Racing Rules Quizzes* is published by the United States Sailing Association (US SAILING). For a comprehensive explanation of the rules, read Dave Perry's *Understanding the Racing Rules of Sailing through 2012* which also is available from US SAILING — 1 (800) 877-2451 or www.ussailing.org

hearing. Use rule F2.2(c) as a checklist.

The written part or "description" of the incident should be brief and should stick to the facts. Again, I suggest listing the important facts and points you wish to make in a rough draft before putting them on the protest form. I like to number the sentences as they refer to the diagram, and obviously the diagram and description should match perfectly.

FILING THE PROTEST

At the outset of the regatta, it's very important to find out where to get the protest forms and where to file them in case of a protest. Don't wait until you're involved in one because things are usually hectic then. Also, as soon as you come in from the race, find out when the time ends for filing your protest. This is critical so you know if you have time to shower, eat something, and just relax, without the risk of missing the cut-off time. Unfortunately, usually you don't. When possible, have your crew or friends put the boat away and contact possible witnesses. When you file the protest, be sure you note *who* received it and the time, and ask them to put the time and their initials on the form, if they haven't done so already. Finally, keep a copy for yourself.

WITNESSES

Good witnesses can be very helpful to your case. The idea behind a witness is to verify the facts you have presented in your testimony. The key attributes of a good witness are: a) they were in a position to see the incident clearly; b) they were close by and watching as the incident developed; and c) they understand sailboat racing (if not a competitor). Obviously the jury should be aware when a witness is associated with one of the parties, such as a crew or teammate, but good juries often learn from these witnesses too.

On the other hand, a poor witness can destroy your case. Don't bring a witness into the hearing who merely told you that they saw the incident and feel you were in the right. Thoroughly screen any witnesses to be sure they understand the protest clearly and that they are definitely on your side. I certainly don't want to imply that you should bring in a witness who has been coached or reflects anything but total integrity, but you must find witnesses who corroborate

Based on *The Racing Rules of Sailing for 2009–2012. Dave Perry's 100 Best Racing Rules Quizzes* is published by the United States Sailing Association (US SAILING). For a comprehensive explanation of the rules, read Dave Perry's *Understanding the Racing Rules of Sailing through 2012* which also is available from US SAILING — 1 (800) 877-2451 or www.ussailing.org

your observation one hundred percent. There often seems to be a feeling that bringing in a witness you haven't talked to establishes some feeling of credibility. It doesn't. You only look foolish and it usually wastes the time of a lot of people. I can't tell you how many times I've sat in a hearing and the jury has had to ask which boat the witness was for. Also, I would suggest minimizing the number of witnesses. Besides the fact that witnesses are generally poorly prepared, keep in mind that when five people see an incident, they may each see it a little differently. The more witnesses you call who saw it slightly differently, the more doubt it casts on your credibility.

Your right to call and question witnesses, including your crew, is stated in rule 63.6. If a member of the protest committee intends to bring their observation of the incident into the deliberation, rule 63.6 requires them to give their evidence as a witness in front of you and be questioned. Although the protest committee is required to hear all witnesses presented by a party to the hearing, it is nevertheless wise to minimize the number of witnesses you call.

PREPARING YOUR PROTEST

The final step is to review your facts and how you will substantiate or prove them to be true. One good technique is to role-play the hearing, with friends acting as the judge and protestee. It is key to prepare yourself for any questions the jury or other parties to the protest might ask you. They might include: What was your crew doing as the situation developed? What conversations took place on your boat and between the boats? How fast were you going? How can you be sure there was an overlap? What were the numbers of some of the other boats in the vicinity? How much time was there between the establishment of the overlap and the initial contact? You should be testing yourself and your witnesses with these types of questions before you go into the hearing. Also review the copies of your protest form to refresh your memory about what you said, and to see if there are any additional points or clarifications you need to make.

PREPARING YOUR DEFENSE

You should prepare a defense exactly as though you were filing a protest. Write down all the facts that support your claim that you were not in the wrong, as

Based on *The Racing Rules of Sailing for 2009 – 2012. Dave Perry's 100 Best Racing Rules Quizzes* is published by the United States Sailing Association (US SAILING). For a comprehensive explanation of the rules, read Dave Perry's *Understanding the Racing Rules of Sailing through 2012* which also is available from US SAILING — 1 (800) 877-2451 or www.ussailing.org

well as the evidence you will use to substantiate or prove your facts. Get all the speeds and distances organized and think through the possible questions. Even if you haven't filed a counter-protest, having everything written out will serve as a good reference. Also, under rule 63.2, you are entitled to see a copy of the protest against you before the hearing begins. Doing this is very important. The hearing room is not the place to start putting together your defense. The protesting boat will be extremely well prepared with all the facts written down and thoughtfully organized. You want to go into the hearing just as well prepared.

To get a copy of the protest, you may have to ask for it. Rule 63.2 requires only that the protest information be made available to all parties, not that it be supplied to them if they have not requested it. As a practical matter, a copy of the protest is often given to the parties when they check in at the jury desk. If that doesn't happen, however, ask for a copy.

One last thought on preparation. Rule 61.1(a) requires that the protesting boat hail "Protest" at the first reasonable opportunity when her protest concerns an incident in the racing area that she is involved in or sees. In all other cases, a protesting boat shall always inform the other boat at the first reasonable opportunity. Be sure to comply with this and to personally notify the other skipper(s) either on the water or as soon as possible after you come in that you are protesting. If you know it, tell them the time and place of the hearing so it will commence smoothly and on time. It is not to your advantage to have the hearing held up or postponed while people look for the other parties. Also, be sure you are on time, even a bit early in case the jury is ahead of schedule, and that your witnesses are standing by right outside the hearing room. Your case can be weakened if the hearing has to be interrupted while your witnesses are being looked for. If you are the protestee, be doubly sure that you and your witnesses are there on time. Jury duty is a very demanding, time-consuming activity, which often requires the jury to be in session for hours at a time. So it doesn't endear one to them when they've given up their cocktail hour, dinner, and probably some much more engaging social event to be kept waiting in the hearing room while the competitor is at the snack bar or elsewhere and unwilling to spend five or ten minutes in readiness to be called.

Based on *The Racing Rules of Sailing for 2009–2012*. *Dave Perry's 100 Best Racing Rules Quizzes* is published by the United States Sailing Association (US SAILING). For a comprehensive explanation of the rules, read Dave Perry's *Understanding the Racing Rules of Sailing through 2012* which also is available from US SAILING — 1 (800) 877-2451 or www.ussailing.org

The Hearing

Rule 63.3(a) makes it clear that you have the right to be present throughout the hearing of all the evidence. Rule 63.3(b) adds that if a party fails to attend the hearing, the protest committee may nevertheless decide the protest.

The rules governing the actions of the protest committee and providing you with your procedural rights are covered in Part 5, Section B, of the *RRS*. If the protest committee, during the course of dealing with a protest, improperly denies you any of your procedural rights under the rules of Part 5, Section B, you have the right to object.

You can either voice your objection at the time, or seek redress after the hearing under rule 62.1(a) when you believe that an improper action of the protest committee has made your finishing score significantly worse through no fault of your own. Note that US SAILING prescribes that the time limit for filing a request for redress from an action/omission of a protest committee is the protest time limit or two hours after the incident, whichever is later.

When the testimony portion of the hearing is over and the parties have been excused, the first task of the jury is to list the facts they have deduced from the testimony. Then, based on these facts alone, they apply the rules and make their decision (rule 63.6). Remembering that in most cases the jury will not have seen your incident or the events leading up to it, the strength of your case lies in your ability to describe the whole scene to them. The more logical, precise, and complete your description is, the better your chances are that the facts will be found as you have presented them.

OPENING TESTIMONY

First the protestor has the opportunity of presenting his case, then the protestee presents his. At this point, the questions between them and from the jury are usually restricted to clarifying what each has said. There will be differences of opinions, usually due to different points of observation. But after listening to the complete presentations of the competitors and witnesses, the jury can usually tell which observation is most credible. When making your opening testimony, keep it brief and speak slowly and clearly. Obviously, this is an opportunity to

Based on *The Racing Rules of Sailing for 2009–2012. Dave Perry's 100 Best Racing Rules Quizzes* is published by the United States Sailing Association (US SAILING). For a comprehensive explanation of the rules, read Dave Perry's *Understanding the Racing Rules of Sailing through 2012* which also is available from US SAILING — 1 (800) 877-2451 or www.ussailing.org

transmit information to the jury more directly, so the diagram and description on the protest form can be expanded on. But try not to add any new dimensions orally to what has already been stated in writing unless you have left something off the form that is critical to your case, in which case mention that you are adding it. The important thing is to focus very hard on the facts you are trying to present and prove. Also, be complete. Omitting a part of the overall picture or filling in details later in response to questions is very unsettling and indicates gaps in your testimony.

USING THE MODELS

When using the boat models, hold your hands so everyone can see what you're showing. If you are explaining that you were two lengths ahead of the other boat, be sure to accurately place your boat two of the model's lengths ahead. If the boats weren't overlapped, don't carelessly place them overlapped; and if the models have booms, be sure the booms are always on the correct side. Here again let me emphasize how important it is to give the exact relationships of the boats, their angles, and their speeds. Remember, if you are going to guess, guess at them before you go into the hearing room, but don't force the jury to interrupt your presentation in order to get these facts. They are absolutely necessary and if you don't know them, your case will be severely weakened. (Another reason for precluding interruptions by the jury is that it doesn't give your opponent any tips prior to presenting their testimony.) Also, don't just start moving the boats around the table. Go through the various positions as you did in preparing your diagram, and go back only as far in the evolution of the event as you feel is necessary. If the jury wants you to go back further, they will ask you.

USING NOTES AND THE RULEBOOK IN THE HEARING

Don't hesitate to bring notes with you into the hearing. In fact, it's a good idea to outline the points you wish to make as well as the possible questions to ask. Also, you should be taking notes while your competitor or the witnesses are giving testimony. You have the opportunity to make a final statement and if the protest is at all lengthy, it is often difficult to recall all the comments that were made. And when making reference to a rule or appeal, don't hesitate to

Based on *The Racing Rules of Sailing for 2009 – 2012. Dave Perry's 100 Best Racing Rules Quizzes* is published by the United States Sailing Association (US SAILING). For a comprehensive explanation of the rules, read Dave Perry's *Understanding the Racing Rules of Sailing through 2012* which also is available from US SAILING — 1 (800) 877-2451 or www.ussailing.org

open the books. It doesn't diminish your credibility, and you'll always be sure to get it right.

QUESTIONS

Before and during the hearing write down the questions you will ask your competitor and witnesses. These should be used for unearthing facts, not making accusations. Also, don't ask your competitor to verify your assumptions, because they are too easily refuted and usually don't have much to do with the facts. During your competitor's testimony, listen carefully for inconsistencies. When questioning your own witness, never ask a question to which you don't already know the answer. And don't feel obligated to ask questions of your competitor or the witnesses. Evaluate their statements, and if you feel that their statements have not been detrimental to your case, don't give them the opportunity to open up new avenues of information.

In responding to questions, there are three basic stages an attorney will advise: First, listen to the question; second, think about it; third, give the answer. It is always important to directly address the question asked. Don't use it as a springboard for adding to your testimony. A good jury will only reprimand you and tell you to stick to the facts in questioning. You'll have the chance to give more testimony later. When answering, it's fair to take some time to think about your response. A thoughtful answer is much more useful than a quick one. Also, no matter how bad a question might seem, don't judge the person asking it or give a facetious answer. Sometimes your competitor might merely want to demonstrate that you don't think clearly in a tense situation. That may be all that's needed to convince the jury that you acted irrationally on the race course. Often a jury member will ask what seems to be an absurd question or might indicate they don't understand the boats or the rules. Some very experienced and clever judges get information by asking questions that might seem way off the track. So always maintain your poise and show you can field tough questions that may even be intended to confuse you.

HOW TO DEAL WITH SUSPECTED LYING

Although protests can sometimes be very disagreeable, my advice is to never

Based on *The Racing Rules of Sailing for 2009 – 2012*. *Dave Perry's 100 Best Racing Rules Quizzes* is published by the United States Sailing Association (US SAILING). For a comprehensive explanation of the rules, read Dave Perry's *Understanding the Racing Rules of Sailing through 2012* which also is available from US SAILING — 1 (800) 877-2451 or www.ussailing.org

take antagonism into the hearing. I think it undermines your case to indicate to the jury that you feel the other person is lying or has acted in an unsportsman-like manner. Some of the very young competitors will sit and roll their eyes, throw their hands in the air, and make all kinds of gestures and noises while their opponent is giving his testimony. Trying to influence a jury by that kind of action is strictly bush league, and a championship competitor should be more poised than to submit to it. Instead, you should focus on a very precise presentation of your own testimony and, if necessary, focus some direct questioning on certain areas of your opponent's story. If your opponent's story is inaccurate or fabricated, it will usually break down somewhere along the line.

FINAL STATEMENT

The last step in the hearing of the testimony is a final statement by each competitor. Focus on the key points and be brief. If you have made notes during the testimony, you'll be able to quickly review the facts that support your case and any other key issues. Never introduce new facts or statements. Also, avoid explaining the rules or implying that if you lose your case it will be a miscarriage of justice. If you suspect your competitor was lying or giving distorted facts, avoid facetious remarks but address the fact that in your opinion your opponent presented a very inaccurate description of the incident. Lastly, state the rule(s) you feel should be applied.

One last word about protest hearings. No matter how objective the jury members are, we are all influenced by people's behavior and the way they present themselves in this type of human interaction. It's to your advantage, always, to establish a good rapport with the jury. The best way is to follow the advice above in both your preparation and presentation. Good jurors will immediately pick up your thoroughness and respect you for it. Also, always take yourself seriously, and especially when around the judges. Horsing around on the water or on shore or becoming a regular in the hearing room with inane protests will lower the esteem of any judge. Keep in mind that as you get nearer the top of the sport, the names and faces of the competitors start becoming familiar to the top judges, and your reputation will become well known. Be sure it's the kind of reputation you're proud of, and you'll get a lot of mileage from it.

Based on *The Racing Rules of Sailing for 2009 – 2012. Dave Perry's 100 Best Racing Rules Quizzes* is published by the United States Sailing Association (US SAILING). For a comprehensive explanation of the rules, read Dave Perry's *Understanding the Racing Rules of Sailing through 2012* which also is available from US SAILING — 1 (800) 877-2451 or www.ussailing.org

Protest Form

also for requests for redress and reopening

Date & time received _____

Received by _____ Filing no. ____

Fill in and check as appropriate

---

1. **EVENT** _____ Organizing authority _____ Date _____ Race no. ____

2. **TYPE OF HEARING**

   ☐ Protest by boat against boat

   ☐ Protest by race committee against boat

   ☐ Protest by protest committee against boat

   ☐ Request for redress by boat or race committee

   ☐ Consideration of redress by protest committee

   ☐ Request by boat or race committee to reopen hearing

   ☐ Consideration of reopening by protest committee

3. **BOAT PROTESTING, OR REQUESTING REDRESS OR REOPENING**

   Class _____ Sail no. _____ Boat's name _____

   Represented by _____ Tel. _____ E-mail _____

4. **BOAT(S) PROTESTED OR BEING CONSIDERED FOR REDRESS**

   Class _____ Sail no. _____ Boat's name _____

5. **INCIDENT**

   Time and place of incident _____

   Rule(s) alleged to have been broken _____ Witness(es) _____

6. **INFORMING PROTESTEE**

   How did you inform the protestee of your intention to protest?

   ☐ By hailing When? _____ Words used _____

   ☐ By displaying a red flag When? _____

   ☐ By informing her in some other way Give details _____

---

7. **DESCRIPTION OF INCIDENT**
   (use another sheet if necessary)

Diagram: one square = one hull length
Show position of boats, wind
and current direction, marks.

This form is based on *The Racing Rules of Sailing for 2009 – 2012*. *Dave Perry's 100 Best Racing Rules Quizzes* is published by the United States Sailing Association (US SAILING). For a comprehensive explanation of the rules, read Dave Perry's *Understanding the Racing Rules of Sailing through 2012* which also is available from US SAILING — 1 (800) 877-2451 or www.ussailing.org

THIS SIDE FOR PROTEST COMMITTEE USE Fill in and check as appropriate	Class _____ Race no. ___ Filing no. ___ Heard together with numbers _____

❏ Withdrawal requested; signature _____ ❏ Withdrawal permitted

Protest time limit _____ ❏ Time limit extended

❏ Protest, or request for redress or reopening, received within time limit

Protestor, or party requesting redress or reopening, represented by _____

Other party, or boat being considered for redress, represented by _____

Names of witnesses _____

Interpreters _____   **Remarks**

No objection about interested party . . . . ❏ _____

Written protest or request identifies incident . . . ❏ _____

'Protest' hailed at first reasonable opportunity . . ❏ _____

No hail needed; protestee informed at first . . . . . ❏ _____
reasonable opportunity

Red flag conspicuously displayed at first . . . . ❏ _____
reasonable opportunity

❏ **Protest or request valid; hearing will continue**   ❏ **Protest or request invalid;
hearing is closed**

FACTS FOUND

❏ Diagram of boat ___ is endorsed by committee. ❏ Committee's diagram is attached.

CONCLUSIONS AND RULES THAT APPLY

DECISION

Protest: ❏ dismissed   Boat(s) _____ is (are) ❏ disqualified from race(s) _____
❏ penalized as follows _____

Redress: ❏ not given   ❏ given as follows _____

Request to reopen a hearing: ❏ denied ❏ granted	**Written decision requested**
PROTEST COMMITTEE	When _____
Members _____	By whom _____
Chairman's signature _____ Date & time _____	Date provided _____

This form is based on *The Racing Rules of Sailing for 2009 – 2012*. Dave Perry's *100 Best Racing Rules Quizzes* is published by the United States Sailing Association (US SAILING). For a comprehensive explanation of the rules, read Dave Perry's *Understanding the Racing Rules of Sailing through 2012* which also is available from US SAILING — 1 (800) 877-2451 or www.ussailing.org

Quiz Index

For a comprehensive explanation as well as the complete text of *The Racing Rules of Sailing for 2009 – 2012*, refer to Dave Perry's *Understanding the Racing Rules of Sailing through 2012.*

Rules Index

By rule title or subject, rule number and page number

About the Author

DAVE PERRY grew up sailing on Long Island Sound. Learning to sail in Sunfish, Blue Jays and Lightnings from his parents and in the junior program at the Pequot Yacht Club in Southport, Connecticut, he won the Clinton M. Bell Trophy for the best junior record on L.I.S. in 1971. While at Yale (1973-77) he was captain of the National Championship Team in 1975, and was voted All-American in 1975 and 1977. Other racing accomplishments include: 1st, 1978 Tasar North Americans; 5th, 1979 Laser Worlds; 1st, 1979 Soling Olympic Pre-Trials (crew); 10th overall, 1981 SORC (crew); 3rd, 1982 Soling Worlds; 1st, 1982, 2006 and 2008 U.S. Match Racing Championship (POW); 1st, 1983 Star South American Championship (crew); 1st, 1983 and 1984 Congressional Cup; 2nd, 1984 Soling Olympic Trials; 6th, 1985 Transpac Race (crew); 1st, 1988 and 1992 Knickerbocker Match Race Cup; 1st, 1994, 1999 and 2003 Ideal 18 North American Championship; and 1st, 2007 South American Match Racing Championship.

Dave has been actively working for the sport since 1977. He has led hundreds of US SAILING instructional seminars in over 50 one-design classes; directed U.S. Olympic Yachting Committee Talent Development Clinics; coached the 1981 World Champion U.S. Youth Team; and given seminars in Japan, Australia, Sweden, Argentina, Brazil and Canada. He has been the Youth Representative on the US SAILING Board of Directors and the Chairman of the U.S. Youth Championship Committee, and has served on the following other US SAILING committees: Olympic, Training, Class Racing and O'Day Championship. He is currently a member of the US SAILING Appeals Committee and a US SAILING Senior Certified Judge. In 1992 he was voted into the *Sailing World* Hall of Fame; in 1994 he received an honorary Doctorate of Education from Piedmont College; in 1995 he became the first recipient of US SAILING's Captain Joe Prosser Award for exceptional contribution to sailing education; and in March 2001 Dave received the W. Van Alan Clarke, Jr. Trophy, US SAILING's national award for sportsmanship. He was the Director of Athletics at Greens Farms Academy, a K-12 coed independent day school in Westport, Connecticut from 1986-2006; and served as the Rules Advisor to Victory Challenge in 2007 (the Swedish America's Cup challenger) and the U.S. Olympic Sailing Team in 2008.